Journal of Biblical and Pneumatological Research

VOLUME 1, 2009

JBPR is published annually by
Wipf and Stock Publishers. 199 West 8th Avenue, Suite 3,
Eugene, Oregon 97401, USA

©2009 by Wipf and Stock Publishers
ISSN: 1944-107X
ISBN: 978-1-60608-932-3

The cover of *JBPR* features professor John C. Trevor's photograph of the Isaiah scroll found in Cave 1 at Qumran and is used with the copyright permission of his estate. The scroll consists of 17 sheets of sheepskin sewn together, being 24 feet long and 10 inches high. The earliest biblical manuscript appears here as it looked in 1948 after being sealed in a jar and unexposed to light for over two thousand years. Dr. Trevor has unrolled the scroll to Isa 38:8–40:28. Lines 2 and 3 in the left column contain Isa 40:3 which inspired the community that produced the Dead Sea Scrolls.

Journal of Biblical and Pneumatological Research

Editor
Paul Elbert
Pentecostal Theological Seminary
900 Walker Street, NE
Cleveland, Tennessee 37320-3330

Books for review should be sent to the editor at this address.

All editorial correspondence should be sent electronically to jbpr@windstream.net or to pelbert@ptscog.edu.

Web site: http://wipfandstock.com/journals/jbpr

ORDERING

Individuals—U.S.A. and all other countries (in U.S. funds): $20.00

Institutions—U.S.A. and all other countries (in U.S. funds): $30.00

Orders can be placed through the wipfandstock.com Web site or by contacting Wipf and Stock directly.

Email: Orders@wipfandstock.com
Phone: (541) 344-1528
Fax: (541) 344-1506

Editorial Board

Twenty-seven scholars in twelve countries serve the critical collaborative editorial process of the *Journal of Biblical and Pneumatological Research*, an international peer-reviewed biblical journal:

Guillermo Acero
Institution Biblico Pastoral Latinamericano, Universidad Minuto de Deos, Bogata, COLUMBIA

Mervin Breneman
Escuela de Estudios Pastorales, COSTA RICA

Christopher Carter
Asia Pacific Theological Seminary, PHILIPPINES

Blaine Charette
Northwest University, USA

Roger Cotton
Assemblies of God Theological Seminary, USA

Andrew Davies
Mattersey Hall College and Graduate School, Mattersey, UK

David Dorman
Near East School of Theology, Beirut, LEBANON

Kay Fountain
Southern Cross College, Auckland, NEW ZEALAND

Jacqueline Grey
Alphacrucis College, Sydney, AUSTRALIA

Jon Huntzinger
King's Seminary, USA

William Kay
Bangor University, UK

Dongsoo Kim
Pyeongtaek University, SOUTH KOREA

William Kurz
Marquette University, USA

Leonard Maré
Auckland Park Theological Seminary,
University of Johannesburg, SOUTH AFRICA

Lee Roy Martin
Church of God Theological Seminary, USA

Martin Mittelstadt
Evangel University, USA

David Norris
Urshan Graduate School of Theology, USA

Finney Philip
Filadelfia Bible College, Udaipur, INDIA

John Poirier
Kingswell Theological Seminary, USA

Janet Meyer Everts
Hope College, USA

Emerson Powery
Messiah College, USA

James Shelton
Oral Roberts University, USA

Rebecca Skaggs
Patten University, USA

Roger Stronstad
Summit Pacific College, CANADA

Robby Waddell
Southeastern University, Lakeland, USA

Keith Warrington
Regents Theological College, Cheshire, UK

Wilhelm Wessels
University of South Africa, Pretoria, SOUTH AFRICA

Contents

Volume 1 (2009)

Contextual Analysis and Interpretation with Sensitivity to the Spirit as Interactive Person: Editor's Explanation and Welcome to *JBPR* · 1

KEITH WARRINGTON
    Suffering and the Spirit in Luke-Acts · 15

WILHELM J. WESSELS
    Empowered by the Spirit of Yahweh: A Study of Micah 3:8 · 33

KENNETH BASS
    The Narrative and Rhetorical Use of Divine Necessity in Luke-Acts · 48

JACQUELINE GREY
    Acts of the Spirit: Ezekiel 37 in the Light of Contemporary Speech-Act Theory · 69

JOHN C. POIRIER
    Spirit-Gifted Callings in the Pauline Corpus, Part I: The Laying On of Hands · 83

ROB STARNER
    Luke: Storyteller, Interpreter, Evangelist: A Review Article · 100

Review of Wilda C. Gafney, *Daughters of Miriam: Women Prophets in Ancient Israel* (Leonard P. Maré) · 117

Review of Richard M. Davidson, *Flame of Yahweh: Sexuality in the Old Testament* (Roger D. Cotton) · 120

Review of Robby Waddell, *The Spirit of the Book of Revelation* (David G. Clark) · 123

Review of Graham Twelftree, *In the Name of Jesus: Exorcism Among Early Christians* (Jon Mark Ruthven) · 129

Reviews of Gordon Fee, *Galatians* (Janet Meyer Everts and George Lyons) · 133

Contextual Analysis and Interpretation with Sensitivity to the Spirit as Interactive Person: Editor's Explanation and Welcome to JBPR

It is a both a privilege and a pleasure to introduce this new biblical journal in the first decade of a new century in a new millennium. The *Journal of Biblical and Pneumatological Research* (*JBPR*) is an international peer-reviewed journal dedicated to contextually and rhetorically minded exegesis of biblical and related texts. Topics include theological and Pneumatological interpretation; the role of spiritual experience within authorial, canonical, and historical contexts; exploration of creative and prophetic activities of *Ruach Yahweh, Ruach Elohim*; and various identifications of the Holy Spirit within narrative contexts. We would also hope to illuminate the influence of interpretive presuppositions and bring to the fore the divine nature and action of the Spirit as a person. The journal thereby hopes to stimulate new narrative-critical exploration and discovery in potentially under-explored areas of research.

Before offering an outline of some issues and concerns this new venture might address, I would first note that this is a very challenging time for biblical studies. It is a time when biblical thought itself, and especially the activity of the Holy Spirit as portrayed in ancient texts, is distorted and dismissed both by secular ideology and by theology tied to unexamined philosophical presuppositions that are subservient to secular ideology. While no doubt this has always been so to a degree, the methodology of exclusive naturalism applied to biblical texts today is particularly intense. Perhaps more so than at any other time in the history of Christianity are Gospel traditions and biblical narrative as a whole being subjected to claims touting them as merely nothing but interpretations, unworthy of being taken seriously as either trustworthy or authoritative. Instead, we are urged toward "a-theistic" interpretations in which the meaning of language must be undecidable. Mistakenly justified by the supposed dawn of a new epoch of relativism, the agnostic philosophical speculation and inter-religious fundamentalism of the past two centuries are now applauded as models for Christian imitation.

Irenaeus, in his battle with those who adapted the teaching of the Lord to their own opinions, once spoke of a skillful artist who portrayed a beautiful image of a king using precious gems. By rearranging the gems into the likeness of a fox, opponents tried to persuade viewers that the degenerate likeness of the fox was indeed the beautiful image of the king.[1] The same issue is with us today *in spades* in the form of unworthy hermeneutical hypotheses—dogma bent on shredding responsible literary and rhetorically minded communication induces readers to construct whatever false and disordered meaning that might appeal to them. This appears nothing short of bizarre when contrasted with the communicative practice of the global engineering and scientific enterprise, or with the study of classical texts for that matter, but now is supposedly demanded of Christendom by a daunting spurt of unexemplified hypotheses culled from secular philosophy which are dismissive of authorial integrity and advanced as if intellectually camouflaged via a new cultural age of relativism.[2]

Therefore, in this regard, as I set out a raison d'être for this new biblical journal, I feel somewhat similar to Alvin Plantinga, who in his overview of Christian philosophy at the end of the twentieth century, began with this observation: "I realize that my paper will be just one more in a flurry of speeches, papers and declarations greeting the new millennium. We will no doubt hear much about how man (and woman) has now come of age.... There will be strident claptrap about how third millennial men and women can no longer believe this or that, how various items of the Christian faith belong to an earlier and simpler time, and so on. There will be earnest calls to take up our responsibilities as third millennial people . . . we must whip our noetic structures into proper third millennial shape."[3] In this time of man-has-now-come-of-ageism or as-we-now-knowism, biblical scholars are urged to conform to insular philosophical claims about the authorial irrelevance of competent and intelligent authors and to the non-existence of objective reality and truth—academically insular claims that I might add are alien to the global scientific community and the scientific method based on experimental findings.

At the same time we are told about the cessation of great stories[4] and the impossibility of moral and spiritual knowledge. On the other hand, *JBPR* would understand

---

1. Irenaeus, *Against Heresies*, 1.8.

2. These unexemplified hypotheses, like claims of authorial irrelevance and of the supposed nonexistence of objective truth, disregard the experimental/theoretical method and critical realism of modern science—which learns truth through discovery.

3. Alvin Plantinga, "Christian Philosophy at the End of the 20th Century," in *Christian Philosophy at the Close of the Twentieth Century: Assessment and Perspective* (ed. Sander Griffioen and Bert M. Balk; Kampen: Kok, 1995), 29–53 (29).

4. Foreseeing the unattractive consequences of the extreme epistemological skepticism and alien

Scripture as a complex but coherent dramatic narrative with underlying coherence and knowledge of Christ available through the person of the Holy Spirit,[5] one person in many persons.[6] Yet now, in an overly rationalistic and presumptuous caricature of reality—not one even remotely based on an authentic and modest understanding of physical reality as revealed by the experimental findings of modern science—Zeus can be mockingly proposed as a possible creator of the universe. In the highly touted new era of relativism, the Holy Spirit is divorced from Christ and turned into a Hegelian *Werkmeister* who roves about amidst the temples and worshippers of gods and goddesses purveying truths appropriately tailored to suit ideological imagination.[7]

---

literary demands often invoked under the rubric of the new age of relativism, Bauckham counters that "Rather than the postmodern story that proclaims the end of meta-narrative, we need a story that once again affirms universal values while resisting their co-option by the forces of domination" (Richard Bauckham, "Reading Scripture as a Coherent Story," in *The Art of Reading Scripture* [ed. Ellen R. Davis and Richard B. Hays; Grand Rapids, Mich.: Eerdmans, 2003], 38–53 [46–47]).

5. See Heribert Mühlen, "The Person of the Holy Spirit," in *The Holy Spirit and Power* (ed. Kilian McDonnell; Garden City, N. Y.: Doubleday, 1975), 11–33 (a translation of Mühlen's "Die epochale Notwendigkeit eines penumatologischen Ansatzes der Gotteslehre," *Wort und Wahrheit* 18 [1973]: 275–87); Ralph Del Colle, "The Holy Spirit: Presence, Power, Person," *TS* 62 (2001): 322–40; and Michael Welker, *Gottes Geist: Theologie des Heiligen Geistes* (Neukirchen-Vluyn: Neukirchner, 2002), 259–313. We question the notion that the Holy Spirit is an "impersonal force" (see my interaction with Jervell in "Paul of the Miletus Speech and 1 Thessalonians: Critique and Considerations," *ZNW* 95 [2004]: 258–68 [267]).

6. Re this expression of the personhood of the Holy Spirit in Christological context, see Heribert Mühlen, *Una Mystica Persona. Die Kirche als das Mysterium der heilsgeschichtliche Identität des Heiligen Geistes in Christus und den Christen: Eine Person in vielen Personen* (2nd ed.; Paderborn: Schöningh, 1967), with a review by Yves Congar (*RSPT* 55 [1971]: 334–39).

7. Aside from the obvious embracing of the authorial irrelevance of biblical writers and the evident opposition to their intentions in this distorted caricature of the Holy Spirit, one can also observe how far removed such sub-Christian polytheistic speculation is from patristic understandings of soteriology. For example, Irenaeus states, "Where the church is, there is the Spirit of God, and where the Spirit of God is there is the church" (*Against Heresies*, 3.24.1) and calls the Holy Spirit our "communion with God" (*Against Heresies*, 5.1.5).

For *JBPR*, the Spirit is not an inter-religious Hegelian spirit-agent or the spirit of another god or goddess as in the theism of Whitehead. Neither is the Spirit of God a social construction or a metaphor for human experience to be replaced by one of Heidegger's divinities or godly ones (*die Göttlichen*) who supposedly relate better to mortals, nor is the Spirit in biblical texts a Kantian supreme being who cannot be experienced.

Instead, we affirm that the biblical Spirit of God is the Spirit of Jesus, a unique and inimitable person united to the church of Christ via divine Pneumatological action as expressed, for example, by Basil, "through the Spirit we become intimate with God" (*On the Holy Spirit*, 19.49).

Christian philosopher J. P. Moreland assesses such intellectually questionable demands that are deeply antithetical to historic Christianity as "the crisis of our age."[8] Similarly Alvin Plantinga, who also rejects the ideological demand against specific theistic knowledge, observes that "in American philosophy we have a technical term for all such declarations and calls and other claptrap: we call them 'baloney.'"[9] In this challenging time of the prying apart of history and biblical theology, *JBPR*, along with biblical scholars like Hanna Harrington and Rebecca Skaggs (née Patten),[10] seeks to press on beyond currently influential secular demands and polytheistic-induced assertions foisted upon the church. We believe that these are not as intellectually substantial as their proponents would have us believe. In attempting to serve the historic Christian faith and the one living and true God (θεῷ ζῶντι καὶ ἀληθινῷ,

---

8. See J. P. Moreland, *Kingdom Triangle: Recover the Christian Mind, Renovate the Soul, Restore the Spirit's Power* (Grand Rapids, Mich.: Zondervan, 2007), 17–88.

9. Plantinga, "Christian Philosophy," 29. Moreland argues that since Christianity is a knowledge tradition, courageous resolve is gravely necessary today as we face an intellectual milieu of philosophical imagination that denies the existence of objective truth and reality in knowing, demanding that there is no non-empirical knowledge, especially no distinctive religious or ethical knowledge (*Kingdom Triangle*, 76–88).

In this regard, we need not fear being swamped by the groundswell of uncritical noise that this philosophical imagination generates. The scientific method of modern science does not, per se, deny the possible existence of non-empirical knowledge based on experimental findings pertaining to space, time, matter, and energy. Such knowledge is simply outside the purview of observation. Denial of the possible existence of non-empirical knowledge requires an anti-theistic or a theistic non-interventionist commitment beyond what science can deliver. Also, dogmatic faith in exclusive naturalism and its popularizations demanding conformity to an unequivocal atheistic methodology—a demand beyond the legitimate domain of the scientific method—can be as fervent as any religious zeal. In such cases, physics is too important to be left to the physicists. This strange anti-scientific philosophical imagination misappropriates and misuses physics to support a pseudo-version of relativism. It is also oblivious to serious suggestions that only the discovery of "new physics" could explain certain observations. The ensuing reinterpretation and depreciation of historic Christianity, truthful knowledge, and divine creative interaction is totally unrelated to physics today.

10. Hannah K. Harrington and Rebecca Patten, "Pentecostal Hermeneutics and Postmodern Literary Theory," *Pneuma* 16 (1994): 109–14. Kevin Vanhoozer also rejects postmodern conditions and argues that Christianity is beyond them in "Beyond Postmodernity: The Recovery of Theology," *The Cambridge Companion to Postmodern Theology* (ed. Kevin J. Vanhoozer; Cambridge: Cambridge University Press, 2003), 162–66. J. P. Moreland suggests that acceptance of these alien conditions is irresponsible and naïve, resulting in the church becoming its own grave-digger (*Kingdom Triangle*, 77); uncritical adoption of these end-of-history philosophical illusions is also critiqued by R. Scott Smith, *Truth and the New Kind of Christian* (Wheaton, Ill.: Crossway, 2005), 154–55, 168.

1 Thess 1:9),[11] we affirm the intent of biblical authors to convey both objective and absolute truth as both historically possible and probable.[12]

We suggest that analysis of biblical texts with a legitimate focus on the personification of the Spirit or on an implicit background of God's spiritual interaction with textual characters may serve to revitalize awareness of the ancient practice of examples and precedents in narrative communication. Biblical texts are unique—never has there been a character like the earthly Jesus, for example, and we affirm a connection between the earthly Jesus and the risen heavenly Lord and Christ who bestows the gift of the Holy Spirit upon disciple-believer-witnesses. These unique documents offer a revelatory witness to knowledge of divine Christology and divine Pneumatology, as well as to the human response in the form of experience.[13] Our interest in Christological experience in no way suggests that we are interested in replacing sound doctrine with experience. We would be both advocates of sound theological orthodoxy and advocates of Christological experience. Contextual interpretive analysis taking full advantage of evidence for rhetorical dimensions of

---

11. As to biblical description of God, John Goldingay, "The God of Grace and Truth" in Murray A. Rae's "Christ in/and the Old Testament," *JTI* 2 (2008); 1–22 (7–11), begins "with the fact that YHWH is God. . . . There is only one God and this God's name is YHWH. YHWH is the only God" (9). Drawing "from the Scriptures as a whole an inference about objective truth," he observes that "since YHWH is God, and Father, the Son, and the Holy Spirit are God, Christians can read the OT Christologically" and further, that "YHWH and Christ have the same personality profile" (10). His argument concludes that "A Christological reading of the OT thus lies in what Christians know about Jesus. Its vindication lies in its capacity actually to illumine the OT—not to impose a meaning on the OT but to draw attention to a meaning that anyone can then see" (11). *We suggest that a Pneumatological reading would also serve to similarly illuminate and that YHWH and the Holy Spirit also have the same personality profile.*

12. With respect to the concept of truth in Hebrew and Christian scripture, Arnaldo Momigliano offers the following theological observation, "Jews have always been supremely concerned with truth. The Hebrew God is the God of Truth. No Greek god, to the best of my knowledge, is called ἀληθινός, truthful. If God is truth, his followers have the duty to preserve a truthful record of the events in which God showed his presence. Each generation is obliged to transmit a true account of what happened to the next generation. . . . Consequently reliability, in Jewish terms, coincides with the truthfulness of the transmitters and with the ultimate truth of God in whom the transmitters believe" (*The Classical Foundations of Modern Historiography* [Sather Classical Lectures 54; Berkeley, Calif.: University of California Press, 1990], 19–20).

13. The study of this congruent experience ensuing from theological or Pneumatological appropriation may be in its infancy, see William S. Kurz, "From the Servant in Isaiah to Jesus and the Apostles in Luke-Acts to Christians Today: Spirit-Filled Witness to the Ends of the Earth," and Beverly Roberts Gaventa, "'For the Glory of God': Theology and Experience in Paul's Letter to the Romans," in *Between Experience and Interpretation: Engaging the Writings of the New Testament, FS Luke Timothy Johnson* (ed. Mary F. Foskett and O. Wesley Allen Jr.; Nashville, Tenn.: Abingdon, 2008), 175–94 and 53–65, respectively.

biblical texts and, when appropriate, of evidence for the possible imprint and implication of Spirit participation as suggested by authors of these texts seems mutually appropriate.[14]

The essence of theological interpretation has been defined as "reading to know God," the God revealed in Israel and Jesus.[15] Given this approach, what might Pneumatological interpretation with an identical intent to know God (including both rational and non-rational knowledge), have to contribute? In making the case that exegesis and contextual interpretation sensitive to Pneumatological features of biblical texts is worthy of more attention—interpretation which makes the fullest possible space for an author's possible understanding and appreciation of the Spirit—perhaps features of texts could be discovered that have lain dormant and unrecognized or that have been obscured by unarticulated presuppositions.

In reading to know God and avoiding the imposition of an ingrained confessional system in theological/Pneumatological interpretation, it would seem that an attempt to recognize a priori presuppositions which could lead to their articulation

---

14. Perhaps, with humility and deep respect, it would be apropos to mention a couple of possible textual examples. As we continue to develop our understanding of the new covenant (see Peter Gräbe, "The New Covenant and Christian Identity in Hebrews" in *A Cloud of Witnesses: The Theology of Hebrews in its Ancient Contexts* [ed. Richard Bauckham, Daniel Driver, Trevor Hart, and Nathan MacDonald; LNTS 387; London: T&T Clark, 2008], 118–27) two fine studies come to mind: Thomas H. Olbricht, "Anticipating and Presenting the Case for Christ as High Priest in Hebrews," in *Rhetorical Argumentation in Biblical Texts: Essays from the Lund 2000 Conference* (ed. Anders Ericksson, Thomas H. Olbricht, and Walter Übelacker; Emory Studies in Early Christianity 8; Harrisburg, Pa.: Trinity, 2002), 355–72, and Walter Übelacker, "Hebrews and the Implied Author's Rhetorical Ethos," in *Rhetoric, Ethic, and Moral Persuasion in Biblical Discourse: Essays from the 2002 Heidelberg Conference* (ed. Thomas H. Olbricht and Anders Eriksson; Emory Studies in Early Christianity 11; New York/London: T&T Clark, 2005), 316–34. Might one ask whether the author's awareness that addressees of the word of exhortation had partaken of the Holy Spirit, and thereby had tasted the goodness of the word of God and the powers of the age to come, could be a heuristic factor in further exploration of such topics? Similarly, we note the following excellent study: Jerry L. Sumney, "The Argument of Colossians," in *Rhetorical Argumentation*, 339–52. Might one again ask whether Paul's awareness of the experiential consequences of readers being "in the Spirit" as well as "in Christ" could be a heuristic factor in exploring further both his choice of meaningful terminology and his argument that readers remain faithful to truthful knowledge about the earthly and heavenly Jesus consistent with and supportive of their ensuing Christian experiences, rather than embracing the teaching of the visionaries?

15. Kevin J. Vanhoozer, ed., *Dictionary for Theological Interpretation of the Bible* (Grand Rapids, Mich.: Baker/London: SPCK, 2005), 24. Vanhoozer sets out what theological interpretation is not, why it is needed, and what it is (19–23). It is not the imposition of a confessional system onto a biblical text. It is needed to lessen the gap between exegesis and theology and to overcome the postmodern tendency to turn exegesis into ideology (and vice versa). It is an effort to interpret Scripture responsibly, in concert with all theological disciplines "with a governing interest in God" and a "broad ecclesial concern" (21–22).

might be a worthy goal. For example, one might ask how narrative-critical interpretation sensitive to connective detail—personification and characterization, plot, story line, repetition, literary cohesion and connectivity (recurring terms and themes), along with clear, understandable, and vivid examples and precedents—composed by an intelligent and rhetorically trained NT author for active readers really fares under the imposition of an *apostolische Zeitalter*, a *Pfingstzeit*, and a *Pfingstzeitalter Anwendung* (an apostolic age, a time for phenomena politically dubbed "extraordinary," or a Pentecostal age with its supposedly unique practices)? Would a NT author be given a fair rhetorical shake if his literary efforts are enshrouded with presuppositions alien to his worldview and communicative intent? Could it be that an *apostolische Zeitalter / Pfingstzeit* style of interpretation is an exclusive method that resists narrative-discursive criticism of its underpinnings and, over time, takes on an ecclesiological life of its own that eventually, perhaps unintentionally, excludes others from the conversation?

One example of this epochal imposition and chasmal separation stands out as something ready for retirement. Heinrich von Baer, as Estonian Lutheran pastor who did a thesis at the University of Griefswald,[16] assumed one of the dominant features of this method, namely that the first Jerusalem Pentecost was a salvific event for Lukan characters (the 120 disciple-believer-witnesses [Acts 1:15]). This was never pretended to be any kind of an exegetical result. The fact that the narrator of the double-work identifies the first recipients of the gift of the Holy Spirit as disciple-believer-witnesses is marginalized. Such similarly supposed salvific events of Spirit-reception, akin to the first Jerusalem Pentecost, are then frozen (and thereby provided literary marginalization) via the *apostolische Zeitalter / Pfingstzeitalter* hypothesis. Such events in Luke's fulfillment of prophecy theme could not occur beyond narrative time under this make-it-fit method. Von Baer advances this interpretive stratagem by simply ignoring one of the clearest examples and precedents of a salfivic event in the first book, namely Luke 7:31–50. It does not appear anywhere

---

16. Heinrich von Baer, *Der Heilige Geist in den Lukasschriften* (BWANT 3/3; Stuttgart: Kohlhammer, 1926). Von Baer resisted the previous wise and insightful narrative work of Hermann Gunkel. The prevailing hidden *apostolische Zeitalter* and *Pfingstzeitalter* presuppositions ruled the day, indeed identically to their previous accommodation by Reformers. One explicit example of their political presence is clearly revealed when Calvin, catering to chasmal separation due to this epochal imposition whose vague make-it-fit duration he claimed "lasted only for a time," overruled his own exegesis at Acts 2:38 by a convoluted appeal (see *Commentariorum Joannis Calvini in Acts Apostolorum, I* [Geneva: Ex officinal Ioannis Crispini, 1552], 30).

in his thesis (it would be inconvenient to try and proof-text it out), enhancing the scheme that the 120 disciple-believer-witnesses were not as identified.

From an ancient rhetorical perspective, the dubious outcome so fashioned is that the examples and precedents of salvation/faith/forgiveness in Luke's second book are retained—they escape the methodological truncation/cessation to be applicable beyond narrative time—whereas the examples and precedents of Spirit reception by disciple-believers in the second book (and carefully foregrounded in the first book) are reconfigured and transformed into curious non-contextual examples of salvation. In effect, these examples and precedents within narrative clarity, continuity, and conciseness are thereby extinguished and entombed via the dominating epochal control. Fancifully, von Baer then invents and imposes three narratively divisive periods or times—artificial disconnections that further distort Lukan *Pneumageschichte* and *Pfingstgeschichte*—onto the double-work to seal the sale of this "interpretive" package. This narratively disruptive and incoherent periodization of times, artificial make-it-fit times for no salvation (the first book), for salvation (the second book), plus a vague make-it-fit time for triggering ejection of the unwanted components of Luke's fulfillment of prophecy theme (before Luke wrote would do nicely). Simplistic tactics so evidently unharmonious with ancient narrative-rhetorical intent, which von Baer never engages, led to a suitable ecclesiological version of *Heilsgeschichte*. Unfortunately, this approach was then essentially imitated and embellished, with other innovative variations, by a long succession of Protestant scholars up to the present time.[17] The lingering effects of this exclusionary method of quasi-historical interpretation, together with its creative variations and reconfigurations catering to the urgings of *Pfingstzeitalter* confinement and encapsulation throughout the NT are with us today,[18] influencing scholars who might otherwise relate to narrative and discursive things differently.

However, also today, theological/Pneumatological interpretation fortunately enjoys far better alternatives. As far as the new journal is concerned, I would illustrate

---

17. In the Roman Catholic and Orthodox sectors of Christendom, such simplistic tactics never took hold. For example, Catholic biblical scholarship over the past eighty years takes little notice of von Baer's thesis. It is seldom mentioned and is not employed. It is not cited in sources of "Apostelgeschichte und lukanische Theologie" identified by Gerhard Scheider, *Die Apostelgeschichte, I. Teil: Einleitung. Kommentar zu Kap. 1,1 – 8,20* (HTKNT 5/1; Freiburg: Herder, 1980), 29–48.

18. A prominent innovative/creative variation of this exclusionary method of selective *apostolische Zeitalter* encapsulation—presuppositionally controlled by *Pfingstzeitalter* demands and artificial past "ordinary/extraordinary" dichotomies—is critiqued by Jon Ruthven, *On the Cessation of the Charismata: The Protestant Polemic on Post-biblical Miracles* (JPTSup 3; 2nd ed.; Blandford Forum, UK: Deo, 2009).

this opportunity with two points. First, in what might become a new era of interpretive progress, I would note with appreciation some foundational work with insights worth considering and developing, beginning with that of Ignace de la Potterie and Stanislaus Lyonnet.[19] The Christian does live and wants to live by the Holy Spirit of Jesus, and we are all interested in trying to open up some new visions of what that could mean. De la Potterie and Lyonnet did groundbreaking work in that regard, and *JBPR* would like to encourage similar efforts. Other notable scholarship in that vein, for example, with apologies for brevity, would be studies like those of Gonzalo Haya-Prats,[20] Roger Stronstad,[21] James Shelton,[22] Robert Menzies,[23] Friedrich

---

19. Ignace de la Potterie and Stanislaus Lyonnet, *The Christian Lives by the Spirit* (Preface by Yves Congar; trans. John Morriss; Staten Island, N. Y.: Alba House, 1971). Perhaps the ethos of this work finds continuation in the magnum opus of Yves Congar, *I Believe in the Holy Spirit* (trans. David Smith; 3 vols. in 1; New York: Herder & Herder, 2005) and in the appraisal of George T. Montague, *The Holy Spirit: Growth of a Biblical Tradition* (4th ed.; Eugene, Oreg.: Wipf & Stock, 2006).

20. Gonzalo Haya-Prats, *L'Esprit, force de l'Église: sa nature et son activité d'après les Actes des Apôtres* (LD 81; Paris: Cerf, 1975); idem, *Empowered Believers: The Holy Spirit in Acts* (trans. Scott A. Ellington; ed. Paul Elbert; forthcoming).

21. Roger Stronstad, *The Charismatic Theology of St. Luke* (Peabody, Mass.: Hendrickson, 1984); idem, *The Prophethood of Believers* (JPTSup 16; Sheffield: Sheffield Academic Press, 1999). An appreciation and critique of Stronstad's other seminal work may be found in my "Spirit, Scripture and Theology through a Lukan Lens: A Review Article," *JPT* 13 (1998): 55–75.

22. James B. Shelton, "'Filled with the Holy Spirit' and 'Full of the Holy Spirit': Lucan Redactional Phrases," in *Faces of Renewal: Studies in Honor of Stanley M. Horton* (ed. Paul Elbert; repr.; Eugene, Oreg.: Wipf & Stock, 2007), 81–107. This analysis finds further expression in Shelton's *Mighty in Word and Deed: The Role of the Holy Spirit in Luke-Acts* (repr.; Eugene, Oreg: Wipf & Stock, 2000). Also, in this area of specialization we hasten to mention the work of the great Lukan scholar Augustin George, "L'Esprit-Saint dans l'oeuvre de Luc," *RB* 85 (1978): 500–42.

23. Robert P. Menzies, *The Development of Early Christian Pneumatology with Special Reference to Luke-Acts* (JSNTSup 54; Sheffield: JSOT Press, 1991). In the first part of this thesis Menzies provides some valuable observations on the Spirit in intertestamental Judaism where experience of the Spirit is often identified with prophetic inspiration, providing solid undergirding for his "Spirit and Power in Acts: A Response to Max Turner," *JSNT* 49 (1993): 11–20.

Horn,[24] Hee-Seong Kim,[25] Gordon Fee,[26] Raniero Cantalamessa,[27] Craig Keener,[28] Blaine Charette,[29] Chris Thomas,[30] Keith Warrington,[31] and Paul Elbert,[32] and the various investigations of Eduard Schweizer, John Rea, Stanley Horton, and George Montague.[33] Over a hundred years ago, William Shoemaker's research specifically set out to draw connections between the Holy Spirit and the Spirit of YHWH.[34] As to the more recent OT area itself we would express gratitude and appreciation, again with apologies for brevity, for stimulating insights to be found in the various investigations of Paul van Imschoot, Alphonsus Benson, Claus Westermann, Robert

---

24. Friedrich Wilhelm Horn, *Das Angeld des Geistes. Studien zur paulinischen Pneumatologie* (FRLANT 154; Göttingen: Vandenhoeck & Ruprecht, 1992).

25. Hee-Seong Kim, *Die Geisttaufe des Messias: Eine kompositionsgeschichte Untersuchung zu einem Leitmotiv des lukanischen Doppelwerks. Ein Beitrag zur Theologie und Intention des Lukas* (Studien zur klassischen Philologie 81; Frankfurt am Main: Lang, 1993).

26. Gordon Fee, *God's Empowering Presence: The Holy Spirit in the Letters of Paul* (Peabody, Mass.: Hendrickson, 1994).

27. Raniero Cantalamessa, *The Holy Spirit in the Life of Jesus* (trans. Alan Neame; Collegeville, Minn.: Liturgical, 1994); idem. *The Mystery of Pentecost* (trans. Glen S. Davis; Collegeville, Minn.: Liturgical, 2001).

28. Craig S. Keener, *The Spirit in the Gospels and Acts: Divine Purity and Power* (Peabody, Mass.: Hendrickson, 1997); idem, *Gift Giver: The Holy Spirit for Today* (Grand Rapids, Mich.: Baker, 2002).

29. Blaine Charette, *Restoring Presence: The Spirit in Matthew's Gospel* (JPTSup 18; Sheffield: Sheffield Academic Press, 2000).

30. John Christopher Thomas, "The Spirit in the Fourth Gospel," in his *The Spirit in the New Testament* (Blandford Forum, UK; Deo, 2005), 157–74.

31. Keith Warrington, *Discovering the Spirit in the New Testament* (Peabody, Mass.: Hendrickson, 2005).

32. Paul Elbert "Possible Literary Links Between Luke-Acts and Pauline Letters Regarding Spirit-Language," in *Intertextuality in the New Testament: Explorations of Theory and Practice* (ed. T. L. Brodie, D. R. MacDonald, and S. E. Porter; New Testament Monographs 16; Sheffield: Sheffield-Phoenix Press, 2006), 226–54.

33. Eduard Schweizer, "πνεῦμα, πνευματκός, κτλ," *TDNT* 6:389–455; idem, *The Holy Spirit* (trans. Reginald H. and Ilse Fuller; London: SCM, 1980); John Rea, *The Holy Spirit in the Bible: All the Major Passages, A Commentary* (Lake Mary, Fla.: Creation House, 1990); idem, *El Spiritu Santo en la Biblia: Un commentarion biblico y exegético* (trans. S. Cudich; Miami, Fla.: Patmos, 2004); Stanley M. Horton, *What the Bible Says About the Holy Spirit* (2nd ed.; Springfield, Mo.: Gospel Publishing House, 2005); George T. Montague, "The Fire in the Word: The Holy Spirit in Scripture," in *Advents of the Spirit: An Introduction to the Current Critical Study of Pneumatology* (ed. Bradford E. Hinze and D. Lyle Dabney; Marquette Studies in Theology 30; Marquette University Press, 2001), 35–65.

34. This initial study is still of interest: William R. Shoemaker, "The Use of 'Ruach' in the Old Testament and of 'Pneuma' in the New Testament," *JBL* 23 (1904): 13–67.

Koch, Wilf Hildebrandt, John Goldingay, and Rickie Moore[35] and in heuristic treatments of the Spirit in Ezekiel,[36] Deuteronomy,[37] Isaiah,[38] and Judges.[39] We would take an active interest in how the Spirit operates in prophetic speech and how it provides specific direction to God's people.[40] We also join the ongoing interest in exploring how and why the Spirit was perceived, and probably experienced, at Qumran.[41]

35. Paul van Imschoot, "L'esprit de Jahvé, source de la piété dans l'Ancen Testament," *BVC* 6 (1954): 17–30; Alphonsus Benson, *The Spirit of God in the Didactic Books of the Old Testament* (Studies in Sacred Theology 2/29; Washington, D. C.: Catholic University of America Press, 1949); Claus Westermann, "Geist im Alten Testament," *EvT* 41 (1981): 223–30; Robert Koch, *Der Geist Gottes im Alten Testament* (Bern: Lang, 1991); Wilf Hildebrandt, *An Old Testament Theology of the Spirit of God* (Peabody, Mass.: Hendrickson, 1995), with a review by Rebecca Idestrom (*JPT* 14 [1999]: 127–33); John Goldingay, "Was the Holy Spirit Active in Old Testament Times? What Was New about the Christian Experience of God?," *Ex Auditu* 12 (1996): 14–28; Rickie D. Moore, *The Spirit of the Old Testament* (JPTSup 35; Blandford Forum, UK: Deo, forthcoming).

36. S. Wagner, "Geist und Leben nach Ezechiel 37, 1–14," *ThViat* 10 (1979): 53–65; Daniel L. Block, "The Prophet of the Spirit: The Use of *ruach* in the Book of Ezekiel," *JETS* 32 (1989): 27–50; James E. Robson, *Word and Spirit in Ezekiel* (Library of Hebrew Bible/OT Studies 447; New York: T&T Clark, 2006), *passim*.

37. Fruitful possibilities for appreciating the intimate knowledge of YHWH and the experience of his presence as portrayed in this narrative abound. This would support the realism of a call to holiness and relationship, as well as the realism of desired obedience to written revelation. We hope that the theology/Pneumatology of divine presence and the repeated significance of establishing YHWH's name might receive fuller attention. For another heuristic perspective worthy of development, see Rickie D. Moore, "Canon and Charisma in the Book of Deuteronomy," *JPT* 1 (1992): 75–92; idem, "Deuteronomy and the Fire of God: A Critical Charismatic Interpretation," *JPT* 7 (1995): 11–33 (16–33).

38. Wonsuk Ma, *Until the Spirit Comes: The Spirit of God in the Book of Isaiah* (JSOTSup 271; Sheffield: Sheffield Academic Press, 1999).

39. Lee Roy Martin, "Power to Save!?: The Role of the Spirit of the Lord in the Book of Judges," *JPT* 16 (2008): 21–50; idem, *The Unheard Voice of God: A Pentecostal Hearing of the Book of Judges* (JPTSup 32: Blandford Forum, UK: Deo, 2008).

40. Michael H. Floyd and Robert D. Haak, eds., *Prophets, Prophecy, and Prophetic Texts in Second Temple Judaism* (Library of Hebrew Bible/OT Studies 427; New York: T&T Clark, 2006).

41. Arthur E. Sekki, *The Meaning of Ruach at Qumran* (SBLDS 110; Atlanta, Ga.: Scholars Press, 1989); W. E. Nunnally, "The Fatherhood of God at Qumran" (PhD diss., Hebrew Union College, Jewish Institute of Religion, 1992); Robert W. Kvalvaag, "The spirit in human beings in some Qumran non-biblical texts," in *Qumran Between the Old and New Testaments* (ed. Frederick H. Cryer and Thomas L. Thompson; JSOTSup 290; Sheffield: Sheffield Academic Press, 1998), 49–80; John R. Levison, *The Spirit in First-Century Judaism* (AGJU 29; 4th ed.; Boston, Mass.: Brill, 2002); idem, "Ezekiel's Vision and the Dawn of Purity," in his *Filled with the Spirit* (Grand Rapids, Mich.: Eerdmans, 2009), 202–18; Jörg Frey, "Flesh and Spirit in the Palestinian Jewish Sapiential Tradition and in the Qumran Texts: An Inquiry into the Background of Pauline Usage" in *The Wisdom Texts from Qumran and the Development of Sapiential Thought* (ed. Charlotte Hempel, Armin Lange and Hermann Lichtenberger; BETL 159; Leuven: Leuven University Press, 2002), 367–404; Alex Jassen, *Mediating the Divine: Prophecy and Revelation in the Dead Sea Scrolls and Second Temple Judaism* (STDJ 68; Leiden: Brill, 2007).

Secondly, as we join biblical scholars like Adele Berlin in developing responsible interpretive procedures,[42] we would also observe a developing analytical approach to biblical texts that could be broadly described as a socio-rhetorical perspective. Instead of an exclusionary method with regard to activities of the Spirit of God in biblical texts that is sometimes tightly tied politically to extra-biblical theories of truncation/cessation/encapsulation, this interpretive approach to textual analysis "applies a politics of invitation, with a presupposition that the people invited into the conversation will contribute significantly new insights as a result of their particular experiences, identities, and concerns. In other words, a socio-rhetorical interpretive analytic presupposes genuine team work: people from different locations and identities working together with different cognitive frames for the purpose of getting as much insight as possible on the relation of things to one another."[43] Given that the heavenly Jesus remembers the life of the earthly Jesus, insofar as our goal of Pneumatological insight is concerned within texts and beyond narrative time, I agree with Robbins that a "key to the power of the argumentative Christian storyline is its comprehensive reach from eternity before the world began to eternity after the world ends. Embedding the story of Jesus in this never-ending story line creates a context where Christians can potentially interpret time in any century as 'Christian time' related to both 'heaven and earth time' and to God's realm outside of time."[44] This approach will have an intrinsic interest in pursuing critical contextual interpretation and should include sensitivity to and appreciation of the distinctive Christological action of the Holy Spirit portrayed in NT documents in light of Jewish and Greco-Roman rhetorical and religious backgrounds, ideas quite harmonious in principle with raisons d'être of *JBPR*.

In concluding my welcome and explanation on behalf of this new biblical journal, I would like to add a brief remark about the implications that may follow from studies touching on the areas and concerns outlined above. As a biblical journal

---

42. Adele Berlin, "A Search for New Biblical Hermeneutics: Preliminary Observations," in *The Study of the Ancient Near East in the Twenty-First Century: The William Foxwell Albright Centennial Conference* (ed. J. S. Cooper and G. M. Schwartz; Winona Lake, Ind.: Eisenbrauns, 1996), 195–207.

43. Vernon K. Robbins, *The Invention of Christian Discourse, I* (Rhetoric of Religious Antiquity Series; Blandford Forum, UK: Deo, 2009), 5. Robbins suggests that a primary task for the 21st century is to engage biblical and related scholars in this inclusive manner: "The goal is not, 'You are included on my terms,' but 'You are included on your own terms'" (*Invention*, 5). This is an admirable and scientifically commendable goal, one that will require critical openness and will take time to accomplish. For now, in this analytic vein, we look forward to Duane F. Watson, *The Role of Miracle Discourse in the Argumentation of the New Testament* (SBLSymS; Atlanta, Ga.: Society of Biblical Literature, forthcoming).

44. Robbins, *Invention*, 50.

open to new ideas, our practice of reading and exploring ancient texts will inevitably have implications, as Richard Hays suggests.[45] He draws out nine implications for practices of reading Scripture in light of the resurrection. Three of these seem especially relevant. I would like to cite these and then add a fourth. Hays argues that to read Scripture in light of this historical event means that we should acknowledge the following: (1) "God is the subject of the crucial verbs in the biblical story. When we read Scripture in light of the resurrection, we read it as a story about the power of God who gives life to the dead and calls into existence the things that do not exist"; (2) "We understand Scripture as testimony to the life-giving power of God. The resurrection of Jesus is not an isolated miracle but a disclosure of God's purpose finally to subdue death and to embrace us within the life of resurrection. 'As all die in Adam, so all will be made alive in Christ' (1 Cor 15:22). For that reason, a hermeneutic responsive to the resurrection can never be a hermeneutic of suspicion toward Scripture's word of promise. . . . If we read the biblical story rightly as a story about this God, we will learn to read it in hopeful trust, open to joyous surprises"; and (3) "The New Testament's resurrection accounts teach us to read the Old Testament as Christian Scripture. To read it this way, as we have noted, does not mean to deny its original historical sense, nor does it preclude responsible historical criticism. Christians have a stake in seeking the most historically careful readings of the Old Testament texts that we can attain. At the same time, however, in light of the New Testament's witness, we cannot confine the meaning of the Old Testament to the literal sense understood by its original authors and readers, for these ancient texts have been taken up into a new story that amplifies and illumines their meaning in unexpected ways."[46]

Fourthly, complementing Hays' three fine insights, to read Scripture in light of the resurrection means also to read it in light of the activities of the same Spirit who raised Jesus from the dead (Rom 1:4). Given that the Evangelists believed the Holy Spirit to be active in the ministry of the earthly Jesus (Mark 1:10; Matt 3:16; Luke 3:22; 4:18; John 1:33) and thus presumably in characters' lives as portrayed by these authors where the nexus of faith/forgiveness/repentance/salvation is recorded, we who now experience and identify with these same events are reading these documents in light of divine action by the same Spirit. Similarly, such a theological/Pneumatological reading would seem to be anticipated by this same Spirit who, as

---

45. Richard B. Hays, "Reading Scripture in Light of the Resurrection," in *Art of Reading Scripture*, 216–38.

46. Hays, "Implications for Our Practices of Reading," in his "Reading Scripture in Light of the Resurrection," 232–38 (232–33).

a consequence of the resurrection (Acts 2:24–33), is poured out by the heavenly Jesus upon disciple-believer-witnesses as well illustrated with literary acumen via a fulfillment of prophecy theme employed in the rhetorically minded double-work we now know as Luke-Acts. It is these documents that can suggest that just as Paul was healed and filled with the Holy Spirit (Acts 9:17), he appears to be a minister of the same early Christian Pneumatological tradition that was applied to him as a disciple-believer when he characterizes his past efforts, "For our gospel came to you not only in word, but also in power and in the Holy Spirit and with full conviction" (1 Thess 1:5). Because of all these resurrection-based divine actions, we can sing "He lives, He lives, Christ Jesus lives today! He walks with me and talks with me along life's narrow way. He lives, He lives, salvation to impart! You ask me how I know He lives? He lives within my heart"[47] (*pace* a demythologized post-Kantian worldview of subjective faith experience and philosophical denial of objective truth, where Jesus "rose in the kerygma" [a notion that Hays astutely rejects]).

So, with Hays, we would pursue critical interpretation of Scripture both in light of the resurrection and in light of experience of grace through the Holy Spirit.[48] With respect to historic Christian faith and these particular realities, Heribert Mühlen, after arguing that the god of the philosophers is not historical (*geschichtslos*), puts it this way: "One need only recall that already in the Old Testament the Spirit of God acted as God's power within history. It is by virtue of the Spirit that God is present among his people. The biblical God not only exists in and unto himself, he also goes out beyond himself; he acts upon the history of men even to the extent of becoming fully involved in it. This indeed occurs precisely through that *dynamis*, that power, which is called Pneuma."[49]

The endeavors that this new journal might pursue can build upon a wealth of excellent scholarship for which we are most grateful. Following the resurrection, in our contemporary "Zeit der Geistgabe"[50] the imprint of the Spirit of the true and living God in Scripture should be responsibly analyzed in all its variety. One hopes to learn things as we go along. In this venture we hope that *JBPR* may afford an opportunity to share new suggestions and discoveries, God willing.

P. E.

---

47. Alfred H. Ackley, "He Lives," (1933).

48. See Donal Dorr, *Remove the Heart of Stone: Charismatic Renewal and the Experience of Grace* (Dublin: Gill and Macmillan, 1978), *passim*.

49. Mühlen, "Notwendigkeit eines pneumatologischen Ansatzes der Gotteslehre," 279.

50. Rudolf Pesch, "Die Gabe des Heiligen Geistes (Apg 2, 38)," *BK* 21 (1966): 52–53 (53).

Suffering and the Spirit in Luke-Acts

KEITH WARRINGTON

Keith.warrington@regents-tc.ac.uk
Regents Theological College, Nantwich, Cheshire, United Kingdom

Introduction

Whereas the Spirit has been associated with prophecy,[1] sanctification,[2] the Kingdom[3] or a wider agenda in Luke-Acts,[4] the relationship with suffering has been insubstantially identified.[5] Into this lacuna Mittelstadt has stepped and provided a useful introduction to and analysis of the purposes of the Spirit in the context of suffering as it relates to Luke-Acts.[6] As a result of a further examination of the relationship between the Spirit and suffering in Luke-Acts, it will be possible to recognize that

---

1. Robert P. Menzies, *The Development of Early Christian Pneumatology with Special Reference to Luke-Acts* (Sheffield: JSOT Press, 1991); Roger Stronstad, *The Charismatic Theology of St. Luke* (Peabody, Mass.: Hendrickson, 1984); idem, *The Prophethood of Believers: A Study of Luke's Charismatic Theology* (JPTSup 16; Sheffield: Sheffield Academic Press, 1999); James B. Shelton, *Mighty in Word and Deed. The Role of the Holy Spirit in Luke-Acts* (Peabody, Mass: Hendrickson, 1991).

2. Matthias Wenk, *Community Forming Power. The Socio-Ethical Role of the Spirit in Luke-Acts* (JPTSup 19; Sheffield: Sheffield Academic Press, 2000).

3. Youngmo Cho, *Spirit and Kingdom in the Writings of Luke and Paul: An Attempt to Reconcile these Concepts* (Paternoster Biblical Monographs; Milton Keynes, UK; Waynesboro, Ga.: Paternoster, 2005).

4. Keith Warrington, *Discovering the Holy Spirit in the New Testament* (Peabody, Mass.: Hendrickson, 2005), 23–34; idem, *Pentecostal Theology. A Theology of Encounter* (London: T & T Clark, 2008), 303-308; Gonzalo Haya-Prats, *L'Esprit Force de l'Église: Sa nature et son activité d'après les Actes des Apôtres* (trans. José J. Romero and Hubert Faes; LD 81; Paris, Cerf, 1975), 197–214; Max Turner, *Power from on High: The Spirit in Israel's Restoration and Witness in Luke-Acts* (JPTSup 9; Sheffield: Sheffield Academic Press, 1996), 428–55.

5. Though see M. Hoek, "An Analysis of the concepts of Suffering and Weakness in the context of the Spirit in Romans 8" (PhD. Diss., University of Manchester, 2006).

6. Martin W. Mittelstadt, *The Spirit and Suffering in Luke-Acts* (JPTSup 26; Sheffield: Sheffield Academic Press, 2004); cf. also the brief overview by Daniel Marguerat, "Une theologie de la souffrance," in his "L'image de paul dans les Actes des apôtres," in *Les Actes des apôtres: Historie, recit, theologie. XXè congrès de l'ACFEB (Angers, 2003)* (ed. M. Berder; LD 199; Paris: Cerf, 2005), 121–76 (152–53).

Luke instructs his readers who live in contexts of suffering and, for some, persecution, that support is available from the Spirit while their destinies are charted by the Spirit. In his gospel, Luke identifies opposition throughout the life of Jesus who ministered in association with the Spirit. In his second volume, he traces the same consequence of Spirit-inspired ministry receiving acceptance but also opposition.[7] In Luke, Jesus suffers; in Acts, his followers suffer. The presence of the Spirit with Jesus in Luke does not result in an absence of suffering; similarly, the presence of the Spirit with believers does not signal a paucity of suffering for them either. As the Son of Man who was partnered by the Spirit suffered (Luke 9:22), so will his followers (Acts 9:16).

The association between suffering and the Spirit is located in the OT. The Spirit is presented as empowering people to be leaders in contexts where people are suffering (Num 27:18; Judg 3:10; Isa 63:11–14) while in times of weakness, the Spirit sustains people and sometimes facilitates their deliverance. The Spirit's companionship in suffering is identified by Hoek as evidence of his "thereness" (Ps 51:11; 139:7; Ezek 37:14; 39:29).[8] As a consequence of his divine presence, the Spirit is expected to bring comfort, sustenance and power, best expressed in the *Ascension of Isaiah* 5:14-15 where the writer describes the death of Isaiah in which he "did not cry out, or weep, but his mouth spoke with the Holy Spirit when he was sawn in half." The role of the Spirit in the context of suffering is also identified with regard to the mission of Messiah, though here again few have commented on this aspect of the work of the Spirit, preferring to identify empowering, initiatory, affirming, prophetic or proclamatory motifs. However, notwithstanding the value of the above emphases, the OT identifies the Spirit's impact on Messiah with regard to providing hope, justice and salvation for those who are suffering (Isa 11:4; 42:2-3; 61:1-3).[9]

---

7. See parallels between Jesus and Paul in Charles H. Talbert and Perry Leon Stepp, "Succession in Mediterranean Antiquity—Part 1: The Lukan Milieu; Part 2: Luke-Acts," *SBLSP* 37 (Atlanta, Ga.: Scholars Press, 1988), 148–79 (174–75). Note that Jesus (Luke 19:45–48) and Paul (Acts 21:26) enter the temple on their entry into Jerusalem; both are seized by a mob (Luke 22:54, Acts 21:30); both are slapped by the priest's assistants (Luke 22:63f, Acts 23:2); both are involved in four trials (Luke 22:26; 23:1, 8, 13; Acts 23; 24; 25; 26); both have a Herod involved in their trials (Luke 23:6-12; Acts 25:13–26:32); cf. Martin Hengel, "Between Jesus and Paul: The 'Hellenists', the 'Seven' and Stephen (Acts 6:1–15; 7:54–8:3)," in *Between Jesus and Paul* (ed. Martin Hengel; Philadelphia, Pa.: Fortress, 1983), 1–29.

8. Hoek, "An Analysis," 23.

9. Hoek provides copious references to this association in intertestamental and rabbinic literature ("An Analysis," 23–29); also Turner, *Power*, 114–15.

The Spirit and Suffering in the Gospel of Luke

The Spirit is involved in judgment (3:16 cp. Acts 5:1-10)

Following the reference to the baptism in the Holy Spirit, Luke provides the adjunctive and perhaps interpretive definition of (the Spirit of) fire as that which cleanses and refines (3:9, 17–18), a concept to be gleaned also from Isaiah 4:4, a verse contextualised in the issue of divine judgment.[10] Although the Spirit is associated with joy (Luke 10:21), he is also associated with judgment; while Jesus is presented as rejoicing with the Spirit in the mission achieved thus far, the basis of that mission is judgment. Whether the motif of fire relates to believers, unbelievers or both, people will suffer because of the Spirit. He burns.

The Spirit inspires those who will suffer (1:15; 4:1-2, 15-19)

These two references to the role of the Spirit are unique to Luke. In 1:15, an angel informs Zechariah that his son, John, will be filled with the Holy Spirit (cf. 1:42–45). More significantly for this exploration of the association of the Spirit and suffering is the reference to the life that John was to live after and as a result of the Spirit's involvement. His was to be a life of simplicity, dedication and sacrifice (1:15), focused on being a messenger (3:4), to be superseded by Jesus (3:16), living in the wilderness (3:2) and preaching a message of repentance and water baptism (3:3) and judgment to the Jews (3: 7–10). His was to be a ministry that was to result in misunderstanding by others about him (9:7–9), rejection (7:33) and uncertainty, as he wondered about Jesus and his own mission (7:18–20). His short mission was to end in arrest (3:19–20) and execution (9:9) and he was to die, unaware of the forthcoming success of the one he preceded. Although his role was uniquely important and affirmed as such by the Spirit (1:67–79), the course of his life was to be challenging as he engaged in aspects of suffering on a number of different levels, specifically as a result of the mission that the Spirit had given to him. He achieved the Spirit-objective in a context of authentic commitment to it but this single-minded integrity was to be associated with adversity. The Spirit who effected the triumph of his task drew him to his destiny through a sea of suffering (4:1–2).

In 4:15–19, Luke carefully records a summary of the sermon preached by Jesus in Nazareth in the power of the Spirit at the commencement of his ministry. As such,

---

10. For other options, see Joseph A. Fitzmyer, *The Gospel According to Luke 1-IX* (AB 28A; Garden City, N.Y.: Doubleday, 1981), 473–75, though he also prefers the association with judgement.

it further identifies "the pattern of acceptance and rejection."[11] In the sermon, Jesus declares good news and identifies himself as the one who will bring it about (4:24). The significance of the reference to the Spirit is to demonstrate that Jesus is not functioning with a human agenda. He is commencing his public ministry in association with the Spirit. His is a Spirit-agenda. Luke presents Jesus as operating in the context or sphere of the Spirit, with the power of the Spirit available to him to use at his prerogative. The message inspired by the Spirit is good news for those who need it most—the poor, the captives or prisoners of war,[12] the blind and the oppressed. The Spirit of power (4:14) affirms and enables Jesus to fulfill these objectives. He is the stronger one (3:16) who can effect these changes for the Spirit dedicates himself to companionship with Jesus. But as with John, his mission, so carefully delineated by Luke (4:18–19), does not meet with long term affirmation. Although there is initial appreciation (4:22), it soon turns into anger, outright rebuttal and physical expulsion from the synagogue and the city, culminating in an attempt to murder him (4:28–29).

Luke has crafted his narrative and its setting in his account carefully.[13] After the remarkable and self affirming events of the Jordan event for Jesus (3:21–22), Luke identifies the genealogical pedigree of Jesus (3:23–38), followed by the skirmish with the devil in the wilderness (4:1–13) that results in Jesus dismissing him and reminding him that he is no mere mortal to be tested; he is, after all, the Lord and his God (4:12). Thereafter, he enters his own home town with the Spirit and is welcomed by all (4:14–15). The long awaited mission is about to commence and thus far, it appears that success and acclaim will be normative, all the more so when the OT is revealed as providing support for Jesus, especially in the person of Isaiah (4:19; Isa 61:1-2), arguably the greatest Jewish prophet,[14] and Elijah and Elisha are associated with him (4:25–27), both of whom were highly honored in Judaism. Thereafter, Luke will record that Jesus fulfilled these commissions (4:31–43). The positive start anticipated is highlighted further by the fact that the quotation, mainly from Isaiah 61:1-2, omits the statement "and the day of vengeance of our God" that concludes the Isaianic passage. This is a comprehensive package of good news with nothing negative to spoil its content.

11. Mittelstadt, *Spirit and Suffering*, 49.

12. I. Howard Marshall, *The Gospel of Luke* (NIGTC; Grand Rapids, Mich.: Eerdmans, 1978), 184.

13. Darrell L. Bock, *Luke 1:1–9:50* (Grand Rapids, Mich.: Baker, 1994), 399.

14. See Robert C. Tannehill, *The Narrative Unity of Luke-Acts: A Literary Interpretation* (2 vols.; Philadelphia, Pa.: Fortress, 1986, 1990), 1:61-63.

However, the final verse in the preceding section that details the remarkable ministry of John the Baptist (3:1–18) should cause the reader to question whether the path ahead will be trouble free, even for Jesus, for his predecessor was imprisoned by Herod (3:20), a strange way to conclude a strategic mission initiated by the Spirit, but one that will be repeated for future believers (Acts 26:10).

As with Jesus, although the immediate response of the people sounds positive (4:21–22), it is followed by the recognition that the one applying this prophecy to himself is none other than Joseph's son, with the implication that he is an unlikely candidate; as Marshall indicates, "the shadow of rejection hangs over the ministry of Jesus from the outset."[15] Although it is possible that the question of the crowds is the cause of genuine confusion but backed by a readiness to accept the unthinkable, that a carpenter's son could be the Messiah, it is more likely a maliciously backed question or at least one rooted in suspicion and a readiness to reject him as a mischievous upstart, the evidence of which is that they seek to kill him before the synagogue service has ended.[16] Luke has recorded thus far the affirmation of Jesus by Gabriel (1:32), by Jesus himself (2:49), the Spirit (1:35), the Father (3:22) and even by the devil who recognises his identity (4:9). Each of them affirms that Jesus is the Son of God, not Joseph. Simeon, Anna, the angels and even the unborn John in Elizabeth's womb have all testified to the status of Jesus and Luke has also recorded that Jesus' ancestry goes back to Adam (3:38). The readers know who Jesus is and the implied question to them is "Why do the listeners in the synagogue misunderstand who his father is?" Misunderstanding on the part of those who listen to Jesus will be a constant companion to him in the months ahead (7:31–35) as it was for John the Baptist (7:33) and the prophets before him (4:24; 13:34; Acts 7:51–52; 28:25). It is no surprise that the few who do understand his identity include demons (4:34, 41; 8:28) while those who are prepared to follow him include ordinary fishermen (5:11), tax collectors (5:27–28), a sinful woman (7:36–50) and those described by Jesus as "babies" (10:21). Most of the people who knew him best and the religiously inclined people who would have been expected to have followed him as Messiah have decided that he is an imposter; as Nolland concludes, "the rejection in Nazareth is a 'dress rehearsal' for the passion."[17]

---

15. Marshall, *Luke*, 190.

16. See also Robert L. Brawley, *Luke–Acts and the Jews: Conflict, Apology and Conciliation* (SBLMS 33; Atlanta, Ga.: Scholar's Press, 1987), 20–21; Mittelstadt, *Spirit and Suffering*, 53–55.

17. John Nolland, *Luke 1–9:20* (WBC 35a; Waco, Tex.: Word, 1989), 200.

However, although the rejection is cruel and painful, it is also startling because Jesus has been anointed *by the Spirit* to preach good news and now the bearer of that good news, and by implication, the Spirit also, are rejected. It is not that the Spirit-agenda is flawed but that suffering is an inevitable element of it and the reader is not to miss this aspect especially where it relates to his/her journey of faith.

The Spirit is presented as one who inspires people to function in a divinely approved and foundationally important way. However, despite the fact that both Jesus and John were partnered by the Spirit and participated in the greatest soteriological act to occur in this world, the achievement was associated with regular experiences of suffering, resulting in antagonism, persecution and execution. The Spirit instituted missions that resulted in adverse trajectories. However, there is a positive note even in the midst of this pain. The suffering of the Spirit-envoys is controlled by the one who has sent them. The prison will not signal the end of the mission of John (he will reappear to witness to Jesus [7:22] and be witnessed to by Jesus [7:24-28]) and similarly, the attempted murder of Jesus will not succeed on this occasion. The Spirit has an agenda and Jesus (and John) will complete it despite the suffering along the way (13:32–33). The message to the reader is that the same Spirit who supervised the often rejected Jesus will also supervise their lives which are also destined to involve rejection (10:16).

The Spirit was involved protectively in the birth of Jesus (1:35)

The role of the Spirit in the birth of Jesus is also recorded in Matthew (1:18, 20) but Luke includes unique information. Whereas Matthew describes the role of the Spirit as initiating the conception of Jesus, Luke presents the Spirit as overseeing the birth. The word used to describe this activity (*episkiazō*) is used in the OT to describe the cloud that rested on the tabernacle (Exod 40:34, 35; Num 9:18) but also to describe the protective presence of God (Ps 91:4; 140:7) when leading the Jews to the Promised Land. The protective role of the Spirit is significant at this most vulnerable stage of the life of Jesus.[18]

The presence of the Spirit was not to ensure that the birth of Jesus was successful or to guarantee the well-being of Mary. Rather, it was to demonstrate the significance of the birth. Nothing like this had happened before and given that the child to be born was God in the flesh, it was essential that such an occurrence should be clearly identified; the presence of the Spirit is the divine marker of a sensational

---

18. See Turner (*Power*, 154–59) for a thorough review of this issue.

initiative. At the same time, it also indicated something of the nature of the mission of the one to be born. The Spirit would provide a sanctuary in the context of malevolent forces that would try to eradicate the child and foil his mission.

Luke's Gentile readers would have been aware of the role of the gods in the protection of their protégés. Two of their most famous writers, Homer and Virgil, had written about the success that had been achieved by individuals as a result of the pro-active and protective involvement of the gods on their behalf. The two main books used in the schools of the era were the *Odyssey* (traditionally viewed as being authored by Homer) and Virgil's *Aeneid*. These stories recounted the lives of heroes battling against the odds, overcoming the perils of the sea as well as natural and supernatural enemies, resulting in their achieving their objective. The supremacy of the gods is proven by their ability to support their earthly protégés against all the obstacles facing them. At the commencement of Jesus' life, Luke presents to his readers information that would indicate to them that this was no ordinary child but one who was anointed by God. What Luke proceeds to do throughout the book is to demonstrate that Jesus is as different from the Greek heroes as the Spirit who is associated with him is different from the Greek deities. He is, after all a "holy" (*hagios*, "different") Spirit. Yet at the same time, the link between Jesus and the Spirit is that the one with the superhuman task can achieve it when he functions with the protection of the supreme Spirit. Although the suffering of Jesus to come is not explicit in this verse (1:35), the extraordinary mission of Jesus and the Spirit's protective presence cause the reader to reflect on the danger involved in the vulnerability of his birth.

The Spirit inspires prophecy that mixes joy with pain (2:25–35)

Again, these verses are unique to Luke though the concept of the Spirit providing knowledge that causes grief is also located in Jewish literature.[19] The role of the Spirit in Simeon was to inspire prophecy. However, although the prophecy foretells the remarkable fact that salvation is also for the Gentiles (2:32), there is pain in the process for many (2:34), particularly Jesus (2:34) and Mary (2:35).

Jesus is destined to cause the "fall and rising of many in Israel"[20] (referring to the division of opinion he will cause), to be "a sign that is spoken against" (a reference to his being opposed and finally rejected) and to be an opportunity for

---

19. m. Hag. Gen 513; 2 Syr. Apoc. Bar 55:4, 7.
20. See Isa 8:14–15.

the thoughts[21] of many to be revealed (2:34–35). The Spirit-agenda has an inbuilt assumption that in order to achieve its ends, there will be suffering, to be referred to again in the words (12:51–53; 19:41–44) and life of Jesus (19:47–48). Indeed, as Luke portrays the painful path of Jesus, the suffering motif is accentuated as the end of Jesus' life becomes centre stage. The parable of the tenants (20:9–18) results in the Pharisees trying to kidnap him (20:19), spy on him (20:20), trap him (20:21); in the Sadducees attempting to trick him (20:27–40); in the chief priests and scribes seeking to kill him (22:1–2); in Satan entering Judas, the betrayer (22:3–4); in one of his disciples, Judas, initiating the betrayal (22:22); in the other disciples arguing as to who was the greatest (22:24–27); in Satan seeking to shake Peter (22:31); in the foreknowledge that Peter will deny him (22:31–34); in the misunderstanding of the disciples (22:35–38); in his loneliness (22:39–46); in his betrayal (22:47–53); in the act of denial (22:54–62); in the physical and emotional assault on him (22:63–65); in the mis-trial (22:66–71); in the trials before Pilate and Herod (23:1–25); in the crucifixion (23:26–43); in the darkness and cry of dereliction (23:44–49)[22] and; in the fact that even his followers watched only from afar off (23:49; also of Peter in 22:54).

Luke's catalogue of Jesus' suffering for his initial protégé, the most excellent Theophilus (1:3; Acts 1:1), makes uncomfortable reading for modern Christian protégés, especially if they harbor hopes that the Spirit's agenda for them will only revolve around pleasant experiences and result in pain-free lives. After all, the Spirit in Luke is manifested in providing people with significant missions and his presence indicates that they will be completed. However, although success is anticipated, suffering was often their escort. Although Jesus had a unique vocation, there is little to indicate from the NT that his followers should expect to lead lives that are fundamentally different.[23] The Spirit does not inappropriately incorporate suffering as part of his agenda for those he guides but it is there and through it, he enables the achievement of the goal. Luke records Jesus describing his life as "my trials" (22:28), *peirasmos* being used in relationship to Jesus and his mission more by Luke than Matthew, Mark and John put together.[24] Where Matthew and Mark merely echo

---

21. Interestingly, whenever "thoughts" (*dialogismoi*) is used in Luke, it always has negative connotations (5:22; 6:8; 9:46–47; 24:38).

22. Given Luke's distinctive portrayal of Jesus' death, it may be reasonably argued that, for Luke, this death is even paradigmatic in some way for Christians themselves, cf. Greg Sterling, "*Mors philosophi*: the Death of Jesus in Luke," *HTR* 94/4 (2001): 383–402 (399).

23. Acts 4:17–18; 5:17–18, 28, 40; 7:54–59; 8:1–3; 14:1–5; 17:5–8.

24. Luke 4:13; 8:13; 11:4 (Matt 6:13); 22:28; 22:40, 46 (Matt 26:41; Mark 14:38).

Luke's recording of Jesus' request that his disciples pray that they should be protected from entering into *peirasmos*, Luke repeats it.

Suffering and opposition are not accidents or malevolent intrusions caused by the devil. Rather, they are part of the Spirit-plan, a plan that will result in the bearer of Jesus into this world being emotionally pierced by a sword (2:35). Luke will have cause to refer to the pain caused by a sword later when he describes the death of Jesus' disciple, James (Acts 12:2). The identity of the pain anticipated for Mary is unclear. Mittelstadt argues that the reference is to the decision-making process taking place in the heart of Mary, concerning the status of her son.[25] However, it is less likely that such a graphic expression is used for this evaluation on the part of Mary, partly because most of the references to Mary indicate that she has realized who he is and her part in the process (1:46–55; 2:19; Acts 1:14), the only other emotion being natural perplexity at a visit from an angel (1:29–30). Furthermore, there is little suggestion in Luke-Acts that this has been a difficult or painful transition for Mary.[26] Rather, it is probable that the imagery of a sword piercing her inner being refers to the death or rejection of Jesus which she will feel like a sword through her own heart.[27] However one interprets the phrase, the fact remains that while there is much that would cause Mary to rejoice as a result of the inspired words from the Spirit, there is pain in the prophecy.

This conclusion to the pericope (2:34–35) should cause the reader to pause and reflect on the section that commences with good news provided by a trustworthy messenger (2:25) and ends with pathos and pain. The Spirit is the inspirer of both parts of the prophecy.[28] An extraordinary revelation of the Spirit is that Gentiles will be given the opportunity to become God's people, but the Spirit knows that such a promise will result in suffering that will even engulf the mother and son who will make it possible.

---

25. Mittelstadt, *Spirit and Suffering*, 43–44.

26. Though see Bock, *Luke*, 249-250; Tannehill, *Narrative Unity*, I, 73; Fitzmyer, *Luke*, 430.

27. Nolland, *Luke*, 122; Marshall, *Luke*, 123; see Bock (*Luke*, 248–50) and Raymond E. Brown, *The Birth of the Messiah* (New York, N.Y.: Doubleday, 1993), 462-63, for a discussion of the options.

28. See also Mittelstadt, *Spirit and Suffering*, 47.

The Spirit may be received as a result of prayer the context of which is felt need (11:13)

The presentation of the Spirit thus far in Luke has provided evidence of his capacity to protect and initiate new life (1:35), to affirm and empower (2:22), to inspire prophecy (1:41–45, 67–79; 2:29–35), prayer (10:21, 22) and preaching (1:15–17; 4:14, 15, 18, 19). It also has identified worthy people as the likely people through whom the Spirit will function (Zechariah, Elizabeth, Mary, Simeon and Jesus). Now, the same opportunity afforded to others to benefit from the inspiration of the Spirit is being made available to the readers also. The Spirit is to offer the same affirmatory and empowering presence as reflected in the lives of Jesus and some of his contemporaries. The outworking of that presence may differ depending on the commission granted by the Spirit, but nevertheless, it is available to those who ask.

That which is important to this study is the context of the verses that detail the reception of the Spirit. Though not specifically related to occasions of suffering, it is associated with need (11:5–12), confrontation in the context of supernatural activity (11:14–23) and rejection (11:29–32, 53–54) while the next reference to the role of the Spirit on behalf of believers is in the context of opposition (12:12).

The Spirit is given to provide support in times of confrontation (12:10–12 also 21:12–15)

Luke records these verses in a conversation between Jesus and his disciples, the core of which relates to opposition (12:1–3), fear (12:4–7), the potential for division (12:8–10, 49–53), the identification of ones eternal priorities (12:13–21, 54–56), anxiety (12:22–34) and preparation for his return (12:35–48). In these confusing times of instability and eventual crisis, the promise is given that the Spirit will provide inspiration. In particular, when it comes to knowing what to say when arrested for their message, Jesus guarantees that the Spirit will inspire them and empower their words.[29]

The Spirit does not remove the suffering but promises to be with believers in those times and to enable them to function appropriately as witnesses to the truth as did Jesus. The suffering though malevolent is not counter productive for the Spirit will ensure that the believers function successfully in it. Luke later identifies occasions when the Spirit does just that (Acts 7:54–56; 13:9–12).

---

29. For a valuable enquiry into the use of *dei* in 12:12, see Mittelstadt, *Spirit and Suffering*, 83.

The Spirit and Suffering in Acts

The references to the Spirit in Acts are generally in the context of his coming into people's lives for the first time or with a new dimension and subsequent impact. What is of particular interest in this exploration of the Spirit is to determine whether the theme of suffering and the Spirit is maintained in part two of Luke's thesis. As in the gospel, there is a mixture of pain and joy, hope and hardship, salvation and suffering. He is introduced by Luke as the one who baptizes/fills, is received by, is given to or comes on people,[30] provides guidance,[31] reveals sin (5:3, 9; 7:51), affirms and empowers people for service,[32] inspires prophecy[33] and supports the proclamation of the Gospel.[34] However, the association of the Spirit with suffering is also identified in Acts.

The Spirit inspires confident witness to Jesus (1:8; 3:12–4:31; 6:10; 7:55; 13:9–11)

A fundamental relevance of these verses is that they confirm that the promises concerning the role of the Spirit to inspire them to speak in challenging circumstances were valid (Luke 12:12; 21:15). This is particularly important because of the socio-religious climate of the day. This was an era of change and insecurity and a time when believers felt increasingly vulnerable.

The suffering of the earliest Christians as recorded in Acts may be understood in terms of its variety including the social divisions in the church, exacerbated by the culture of the day,[35] the marginalization of the believers by the State (21:33; 24:27), Graeco-Roman religions (19:23-29) and philosophies (17:17-33), as well as Jewish abuse (2:13), rejection (13:8, 45; 14:2) and persecution,[36] socio-economic problems

---

30. 1:5; 2:4, 33, 38; 5:32; 8:15–19; 9:17; 10:44, 45, 47; 11:15, 16; 19:2, 6.

31. 1:2, 16; 4:25; 8:29; 10:19; 11:12; 13:4; 15:28; 16:6, 7; 20:22, 23; 28:25.

32. 6:3, 5; 8:39; 10:38; 13:2; 20:28.

33. 2:17, 18; 11:28; 19:6; 21:4, 11.

34. 1:8; 4:8, 31; 6:10; 7:55; 9:31; 11:24; 13:9, 52; cf. Warrington, *Discovering the Spirit*, 51–74.

35. 8:14; 10:9–11:18 (esp. 10:15, 22, 28–29, 34–35, 45; 11:1–3, 17–18).

36. 4:3; 5:17–18, 40; 6:11–13; 7:54–60; 8:2-3; 9:23–24, 29; 11:19; 12:1–3; 13:50; 14:4–5, 19; 16:19–25; 17:6–7; 18:5–6, 12–13, 17; 20:3; 21:27–36; 22:22–23; 23:2, 12–15; cf. Scott Cunningham, *"Through Many Tribulations": The Theology of Persecution in Luke-Acts* (JSNTSup 142; Sheffield: Sheffield Academic Press, 1997), 337-342; Ernst Bammel, "Jewish Activity Against Christians in Palestine According to Acts" in *The Book of Acts in its First Century Setting. Volume 4. Palestine Setting* (ed. Richard Bauckham; Carlisle, UK: Paternoster, 1995), 357-364; also Brian Rapske, *The Book of Acts in its First Century Setting. Volume 3. Paul in Roman Custody* (Carlisle, UK: Paternoster, 1994), 115-435.

(11:28), sickness,[37] demonic oppression (16:18), death (9:37; 12:2), misfortune (27:20, 41; 28:3) fear (9:26) and internal dissension.[38] Furthermore, suffering was not unexpected for it had been prophesied by Jesus[39] and was a theme of prophecy in the early church.[40]

Increasingly excluded by Jew and Gentile alike, the support of the Spirit from the moment they became Christians was a welcome encouragement and one that resulted in an anticipation of provision for their future lives. The first evangelistic sermon that results in the joy of 3000 becoming believers (1:41) was in response to mocking of the opposition (1:13) while the last recorded sermon to unbelieving Jews (28:17-28) was as a result of Paul being arrested and sent to Rome. Nevertheless, as demonstrated by the final word of Acts, *akōlutōs*, Paul will achieve his objective "unhindered" even though the backdrop is the arrest of Paul, a storm, a shipwreck, the danger of being executed and a snake bite.[41] The commencement and conclusion of the lives of the believers may involve suffering, but the Spirit will use it to achieve his will.

1:8

Although this verse is rightly recognized by many as providing a remarkable promise for the potential of the Gospel being presented to the world, its original hearers may have viewed such a prospect with rather less enthusiasm than moderns. The city of Jerusalem and the region of Judea were inhabited by Jews who had not proved themselves to be ready listeners to Jesus; the Samaritans were their enemies[42] and the ends of the earth were to be identified with areas that signaled the unknown with all the challenges that they would bring to would-be witnesses of Jesus. This was a challenging vocation and one that needed the inspiration and empowering of the Spirit to enable them to undertake it at all, let alone to do it successfully. The provision of

---

37. 3:2; 5:16; 9:33; 14:8; 28:8.

38. 6:1; 15:1–5, 39; 21:20–26.

39. Luke 12:11; 49–53; 21:12–28.

40. Acts 14:22; 20:23, 29–30; 21:4, 11–14.

41. See further Daniel Marguerat, "The Enigma of the Silent Closing of Acts," in *Jesus and the Heritage of Israel: Luke's Narrative Claim upon Israel's Legacy* (ed. David P. Moessner; Harrisburg, Pa.: Trinity, 1999), 284–304.

42. Hans-Josef Klauck, *Magic and Paganism in Early Christianity* (trans. Brian McNeil; Edinburgh: T & T Clark, 2000), 14, observes that "Samaria was a transition zone, geographically and religiously speaking, from Judaism to paganism."

the Spirit is to be contextualized in the challenging nature of the commission. He will inspire people who will fulfill his missions for them despite the suffering related to their being completed.

3:12–4:31

The earliest chapters of Acts contain a great deal of information that illustrate the rapid progress of the Gospel, though the first recorded healing results in the now familiar suffering that is associated with the missions of envoys of the Spirit. The response to the questions of the crowd that follows the healing of the paralysed man (3:1–10) includes a reference to the suffering of Jesus (3:18) and the danger of rejecting the prophets of God (3:22–23). This is followed quickly by the arrest and imprisonment of the apostles (4:3) and a defence to a more strident set of questions by the High Priest, elders and scribes of Jerusalem in which Peter again refers to the fact that Jesus was rejected (4:10–11), concluding with threats against them by the religious parties (4:21, 29). The Spirit who empowered them (Acts 1:8; 5:32) did so because of these and other challenges to come, as revealed by the Spirit in the OT (4:25). The promise to inspire those he commissions (Luke 12:11–12) is fulfilled in their experience (4:8) and affirmed by the opposition who recognise their boldness and eloquence, despite their being uneducated and ordinary men (4:13). Their confidence in their words is due to the Spirit-source on whom they rely (4:31). Because of him, the level of suffering will not obstruct their ongoing witness though neither will the Spirit necessarily remove it.

6:10; 7:55

These verses are located in the beginning and end of Stephen's speech before his accusers. In his defense, the theme of the rejection is noted (7:9, 35, 39) and focused on more specifically with regard to his hearers who are identified as those who "always resist the Holy Spirit" (7:51). Luke addresses the issue of suffering experienced not just by those who are commissioned by the Spirit but also by the Spirit himself who is "resisted" by people.

Stephen follows in the footsteps of the Spirit-inspired Jesus (cf. Luke 4:18, 28–29). It is not so much that Stephen imitates Jesus but that he continues the ministry of Jesus.[43] Both are led by the Spirit, both are accused with the same charges concern-

---

43. Cunningham, *Through Many Tribulations*, 206; David P. Moessner, "'The Christ Must Suffer, The Church Must Suffer': Rethinking the Theology of the Cross in Luke-Acts", in *SBLSP* 29 (ed. David

ing the temple (Luke 21:6; Acts 6:13–14) and both die a martyr's death. The suffering of Stephen is not illegitimate or a sign that the devil has won a battle. Rather, it more closely accentuates his being a follower of Jesus and preludes the conversion of Saul and the extended preaching of the Gospel (8:4).

The testimony of Stephen is both a warning and an encouragement. Stephen functions as an example of a believer who was led by the Spirit (Acts 6:5, 10; 7:55). Although there is a passing reference to the fact that he achieved signs and wonders (6:8), the immediate aftermath to the reference to Stephen's appointment as one of the Seven is that he experienced opposition followed by martyrdom. The suffering was neither illegitimate nor symptomatic of weakness. Suffering has been chosen as the way for Stephen to meet Jesus. The message to the readers is clear. To be led by the Spirit assumes the possibility, indeed probability, of suffering.

His witness was empowered by the Spirit (6:10) but it resulted in his death at the hands of those to whom he witnessed. It is a painful lesson to be learnt that not always does Spirit-anointed preaching result in converts. At the same time, this limited success is not presented as being a failure for not only was Saul a witness to it but also at the end of the sermon (7:55), Stephen is described as being "full of the Holy Spirit" (cp. 6:5, 8) as a result of which, he sees the Son of Man standing at the right hand of God,[44] as if to welcome him. The same Spirit, who enabled Stephen to see heaven, also enabled him to face death.[45]

13:9–11

After Luke records that Paul is filled with the Spirit, Paul confronts Elymas, a magician, and blinds him. The Spirit functions here in judgement on one who is opposing the preaching of the Gospel. It is not clear why the Spirit initiates such an act on this occasion and not elsewhere where there has been opposition to the Gospel and Luke does not provide a reason. However, to witness to one's faith in Jesus in the

---

J. Lull; Atlanta, Ga.: Scholars Press, 1990), 165–95; Andrew C. Clark, *Parallel Lives: The Relation of Paul to the Apostles in Lucan Perspective* (Paternoster Biblical Monographs; Carlisle, UK; Waynesboro, GA: Paternoster, 2001), 177–183, 262–267; Tannehill, *Narrative Unity*, I, 83; William H. Shepherd, *The Narrative Function of the Holy Spirit as a Character in Luke-Acts* (SBLDS 147; Atlanta, Ga.: Scholars Press, 1994), 175–79

44. Whether this is to indicate a legal stance on behalf of Stephen by Jesus or whether he is ready to welcome him to heaven is uncertain. What is of fundamental importance to the readers (and Stephen) is that the Spirit-inspired Stephen is also being watched by Jesus; his suffering, though inevitable, is not being missed by the Judge of the world and the one who he is seeking to follow and emulate.

45. Charles K. Barrett, *The Acts of the Apostles* (2 vols.; ICC; Edinburgh: T & T Clark, 1994), 1:382.

first century world was to put oneself in the position of receiving ridicule, opposition and even death. The ability to engage in evangelism therefore was not for the fainthearted. The promise of the Spirit was not that conflict would be eradicated but that the necessary resources to facilitate witness would be made available. Success was not always guaranteed but the resourceful Spirit was.

The Spirit is given to people who have been commissioned to suffer (9:16–17)

S(P)aul receives the Spirit after he has been chosen by God to serve him. Although the Spirit does elsewhere affirm membership in the family of God, that does not appear to be the focus of this narrative. Rather, suffering is identified as a major part of Saul's calling (9:16), an aspect that he will affirm himself (14:22) and a reality that will be referred to a few verses later by Luke when he reveals that a plot to kill S(P)aul resulted in his having to leave Damascus secretly at night (9:23), the first of many such occurrences.[46] Ananias need not fear meeting Saul, as a result of the suffering he has caused the believers (9:13–14) because the Lord himself (note the emphatic *egō*… "I will show him how much he *must (dei)* suffer…") is to reveal some of the suffering that he is to undergo.[47]

The Spirit prepares people for suffering (11:28; 19:21; 20:22–23, 28; 21:4, 11)

On three occasions, Luke records prophecies which result in warnings of challenging events to come. It is noteworthy that the Spirit inspires knowledge about these painful events though does not remove them.

11:28

Through Agabus, the Spirit reveals that a great famine is to occur (11:29–30). As a result of this warning, the believers sent help to those in Judea. The Spirit is identified as inspiring believers to care for each other in contexts of suffering.

---

46. 13:50; 14:4–6, 19; 16:19–24; 17:5, 32; 18:6; 19:23–40; 21:30–36; 23:12–15; 27:14–28:5.

47. Barrett (*Acts*, I, 457) suggests that "Luke is caught between two motivations, on the one hand to show how much Paul was prepared to suffer for Christ, on the other to show the power of God to deliver him from suffering." However, Luke is not demonstrating Paul's readiness to suffer or the Spirit's role in delivering Paul from suffering. Rather, Luke instructs the readers that suffering is part of the Spirit's agenda for Paul. That which the rest of the story is to reveal is whether Paul will be willing to follow this agenda; see also Marguaret, "L'image de paul," 121–54.

20:22–23 (19:21), 21:4–11

Paul testifies that the Spirit has bound him (*dedemenos*), with the implication that he has been impelled by the Spirit.[48] Elsewhere in Acts, the term and its cognates are used to refer to physical captivity and imprisonment of believers (9:2, 21; 12:6; 21:10, 11, 33; 22:5; 24:27). Although the Spirit is not imprisoning Paul, the effect of his commissioning is that actual imprisonment is forthcoming, as clarified in the next verse. His is a Spirit-charted journey that will involve suffering.[49] Luke does not reveal why the Spirit reveals this information to Paul but the reader is under no illusion that Paul, in treading the path to Jerusalem as led by the Spirit (19:21; 20:22), is, as Stephen, following in the path of Jesus who also "set his face to go to Jerusalem" (Luke 9:51).[50]

In 21:11, Agabus prophesies concerning Paul's fate in Jerusalem that will result in his being bound (repeated in verse 10, 11), arrested and placed in the hands of the Gentiles;[51] from 23:16 through to end of the book, Paul's journey to Rome, largely in the hands of Gentiles, is detailed by Luke, the "binding" being fulfilled in 21:33. The *binding* of Paul by his captors is to be understood as a consequence of his first being *bound* by the Spirit. Any suffering the former caused is subsequent to the commissioning of Paul by the Spirit. As Tannehill notes, "his arrest and trials are not an unexpected interruption of his plans but a part of what he must face to complete his ministry."[52] The Spirit-agenda is thus again identified with suffering.

That which is important for this exploration of the Spirit in Luke-Acts is again to note the association of the commission of the Spirit with suffering. As Mittelstadt notes, "Paul, in response to the multiple witness of the Spirit, willingly embraces imprisonment and its sufferings as a divine calling."[53] This was announced at the commencement of his mission in association with the Spirit (9:16–17) and now also, immediately prior to his final journey that will lead to Rome.

---

48. Also Barrett, *Acts*, 2:970.

49. Joseph A. Fitzmyer, *The Acts of the Apostles* (AB 31; New York, N.Y.: Doubleday, 1998), 677.

50. Tannehill, *Narrative Unity*, 2:240, 259.

51. Although Agabus in 21:11 states that Paul will be bound by the Jews, that is actually done by the Gentiles (22:30). It may be that the latter was also done by the Jews also though Luke chooses not to record this. It is also possible that part of the prophecy was inaccurate as appears to be the prophecy (or its interpretation) referred to in 21:4.

52. Tannehill, *Narrative Unity*, 2:266.

53. *Spirit and Suffering*, 124.

Sufferings, whether for Paul, the Ephesian elders, or the believers as a whole are no surprise to the Spirit. It is not to be assumed that the suffering is to be understood as illegitimate or unexpected as far as the Spirit of Jesus is concerned. He, who is in charge of all believers and their commissions, is also in charge of their destinies.

20:28

Paul exhorts the leaders of the church at Ephesus to remember their role as those who care for the believers. He does this by reminding them of two issues. Firstly, they have been commissioned by the Spirit and secondly, "fierce wolves" are to attempt to create havoc in the church. The potential to deal with the latter is strictly associated with the resources available from the former. Paul reminds the leaders of the source of the Spirit available to them, enabling them and equipping them to complete their commissions albeit in malevolent contexts.

Implications

1. The Spirit, who is associated with many aspects of Christian spirituality, is also linked to the issue of suffering. He is the Spirit not only of power and triumph but also of power and triumph through suffering. The power anticipated in 1:8 should be contextualized in the suffering associated with the witness to the Gospel as reflected in the rest of Acts. Praying for more power needs to be recognized as simultaneously calling for more opportunities to exhibit it while embracing challenging situations.

2. The concept of suffering is redeemed by the Spirit as a valuable and integral element of the development of the mission of a believer.

3. That the Spirit does not remove suffering may be significant in instructing believers to accommodate it into their lives with fortitude and joy, knowing that it was such for the prophets of the OT, the spiritual champions of the NT (including Peter, Paul and Stephen) and Jesus himself.

4. Although the message of Acts is that the Gospel triumphs, it is in association with the fact that it does so through suffering. More particularly, the Spirit, who sets the agenda for the development of the church and assures that it will succeed, does so on a route often categorized by opposition and suffering. God is not presented as removing or even lessening the suffering or removing believers from it; indeed, it appears to increase (in the form of persecution) precisely

because they are believers. Luke has two messages. The one is that the Spirit is supreme and will fulfill his plans; the other is that suffering is often the normal (and, by implication, chosen) route for this to occur.[54]

5. It is to be expected that the Gospel will be opposed and that its witnesses will be rejected. To assume a smooth reception by unbelievers is not reflected in the writings of Luke or the experiences of the early Church leaders. The persecuted church is the norm; the church that is not suffering is therefore a cause of wonder or concern. Asking the Spirit to enable believers whilst removing them from suffering is inappropriate; asking for Spirit-power in order to engage in suffering for the Gospel is to emulate the life of Jesus and the greatest leaders of the early church whose prayers were answered in this regard, for some at the cost of their lives.

6. The Spirit-worldview is different to that of many believers today who assume a right to happiness and who expect God to infiltrate their lives with regular pleasant experiences. The notion that God could use suffering in their lives as an instructive and developmental aid is a shocking and even abhorrent notion to many believers. However, the experiences of the believers in Acts do not fit the mould of such a misguided view. What is of greater concern is that the experiences of the early believers appear to be intended to be normative and motivated according to the designs of the Spirit. Somewhere along the way, the role of the Spirit in association with suffering has got lost, to such an extent that now, rather than suffering being viewed as a channel through which the Spirit chooses to effectively empower believers, it is viewed as a channel through which the devil manifests himself and which is therefore to be resisted at all costs.

7. Western believers have yet another reason to consider and learn from the experiences of those believers, mainly living in non-Western countries, who are experiencing phenomenal growth in the context of suffering. Their life trajectories are more in line with those instituted by the Spirit for the believers in the early church.

---

54. Also Beverly R. Gaventa, "Toward a Theology of Acts: Reading and Rereading," *Int* (1988), 146–157.

Empowered by the Spirit of Yahweh: A Study of Micah 3:8

WILHELM J. WESSELS

wessewj@telkomsa.net
University of South Africa, Unisa 0003, South Africa

Power plays a role in all societies. This is clearly also the case in Israel and Judah. Within the societies of Israel and Judah the prophets formed part of the power structures. Prophets not only had powerful positions in the society, but were people. The book of Micah contains a clear portrayal of power abuse; but it is not only about power but also about powerlessness. Chapters 2 and 3 spell out how powerful leaders abused their power speaking powerful words. Prophets however concerned themselves in particular with the abuse of power. In this regard Micah is a good example of a prophet confronting addressing the issue of power abuse in his society over powerless people; and chapter 3 also shows how, on the other hand, religious functionaries (prophets, priests, seers, diviners) who had lost the favour of Yahweh were powerless against a prophet empowered by the Spirit of Yahweh to exercise a forceful prophetic ministry (Micah 3:8). Then, too, power must remain within ethical bounds if it is not to degenerate into power abuse. Micah states clearly that power must promote justice and righteousness. If it does not, it is not to the advantage of society.

In all societies, certain people fulfil leadership roles. In some instances these roles are obtained by virtue of natural leadership abilities, in others by being elected to leadership positions or even by seizing them. All leadership positions confer forms of power on the individuals concerned. Leadership structures might differ from one society to another: indeed, a variety of leadership models are functioning in different societies—whether political leadership (both local and international), religious leadership, family and home leadership or leadership in work-related settings, to mention only a few. Power seems to be a necessary ingredient in guaranteeing an organised society. Power is therefore not a negative component in itself, but the abuse of power can have destructive consequences.

The problem I would like to investigate is the issue of power as it relates to people in positions of leadership, in particular the prophets. In this article I propose to indicate that, in the societies of Israel and Judah, some of the major leadership structures were of a political and religious nature. In the political arena, the kings and tribal leaders played important roles. In the religious sphere, the most prominent leadership positions were held by the prophets and priests. These leadership positions showed clear evidence of power. Interestingly, the prophet Micah (in Micah 3:8) found it necessary to define his own position as a prophet of Yahweh in terms of power.

The focus of the present study is on the issue of power and leadership as it functions in societies such as Israel and Judah. I propose to demonstrate the necessity for power. It will be necessary to briefly discuss power as a phenomenon. It will also, however, be important to look at the danger of power abuse and the resulting conflict. A final step will be to narrow the focus on power and leadership to the sphere of religion, looking at the question of power and prophets and particularly the instance in Micah 3:8.

Power as Phenomenon

Power is a force or an influence exercised on something or someone to cause an effect. There are many examples of power as a negative force or influence. Abuse of power often results in acts of violence or emotional exploitation. Power however needs not be negative or experienced as negative, since is a necessary component to achieve something or get things or people in motion.[1] In this regard power is an essential ingredient in a society. Power in the positive and negative sense of the word was prevalent in Israelite and Judean societies through the ages. It was not different in the time of the prophet Micah in the eighth century BCE.[2]

In the case of the book of Micah, power issues are related to the leadership in the society. In this regard it concerns the political and the religious leadership. Power in this instance, as is the case in many instances, was inherent in the privileged positions these leaders held in society.[3] The big concern in Micah's society was the fact

---

1. "Power as Necessity" in *The Essentials of Power, Influence and Persuasion* (W. J. D. Bliss, series advisor; Business Literacy for Human Resource Professionals; Boston, Mass.: Harvard Business School, 2006), 21–24.

2. Wilhelm J. Wessels, "Conflicting Powers: Reflections from the Book of Micah," *OTE* 10/3 (1997): 528–44.

3. Robert N. Lussier and Christopher F. Achua, *Leadership: Theory, Application, Skill Development*

that people in positions of religious leadership gave backing to political and civil leaders in their abuse of power. Ordinary people, especially people without rights—the widows and the orphans, were the victims of power abuse. The social structures in the Judean society became channels of power abuse. Religious ideals such as the eternal Davidic kingship, Zion and the temple took on ideological tendencies. It had extremely negative consequences for those who became victims of the uncritical and arrogant application of these ideological ideas.

Power as indicated resides in people, ideas and structures. Individuals as well as groups can use and abuse power. However besides power being situated in people, literary text can also be a means of exercising power. In this regard we can refer to the power of the word. Words can be uttered in the public space or it can be written down to become more fixed texts.[4] This is one of the most powerful ways of promoting ideas which will have an effect on people's thoughts and actions. Prophets in particular used prophecy (prophetic words) to convey important messages received from a divine source. The above-mentioned authors argued that the prophetic enactment of delivering messages were powerful in the moment of the performance. But they have also convincingly argued that once these prophetic utterances were moulded into literary texts, these words received new meaning because of the new context it is put in. Though there is a link with the "original" prophetic performance, within the new literary context, new meaning is birthed. I will argue this at a later stage in the article when discussing the text of Micah, in particular 3:8.

One cannot however speak about power, especially within a religious context, without also discussing measures curtailing the abuse of power. Two important aspects worth mentioning are ethics and ideological criticism. Ethics has to do with religious and social values.[5] It serves as a means of putting boundaries to ideas and actions. The prophets and the priests were the two main parties responsible for setting religious-ethical norms and promoting ethical ideas within the Israelite society.[6]

(Manson, Ohio: Thompson South-Western, 22004), 102.

4. William Doan and Terry Giles, *Prophets, Performance and Power: Performance Criticism of the Hebrew Bible* (New York: T&T Clark, 2005), 2–5.

5. Bruce C. Birch has written an excellent article, "Old Testament Ethics," in *The Blackwell Companion to the Hebrew Bible* (ed. Leo G. Perdue; Blackwell Companions to Religion 3; Oxford, UK/ Malden, Mass.: Blackwell, 2005), 293–307, in which he discusses the meaning of OT ethics, problematic issues, the community foundation of OT ethics, divine reality and the bases of OT ethics, and finally, trajectories of OT ethics.

6. Cf. Duncan B. Forrester, "Social justice and warfare," in *The Cambridge Companion to Christian*

Ideas should also be scrutinized by means of ideological criticism. The concept ideology is difficult to define, but as Brueggemann has indicated, it has to do with "... a communal shared meaning," "... a mode of 'social construction of reality.'"[7] Stiebert remarks that "Ideological criticism seeks to point out the political nature of either *texts* or *interpreters of texts,* or both."[8] Several scholars have discussed the notions of ideas becoming ideological in nature and the necessity to unveil and counter negative ideologies.[9] When power comes in the picture, ideological criticism is of the utmost importance to expose the possible abuse of power. This is in particular relevant for the discussion of power in the society of the prophet Micah.

Discussion of Micah 3:8

Micah 3:8 forms part of the more comprehensive unit 3:1–12. This pericope starts with a clear introductory sentence and ends with a sentence indicating the outcome of matters in verse 12 that marks it off from the following pericope.[10] The passage is cohesive in content and may be subdivided into 3:1–8 and 3:9–12. Verses 1 and 9 both start with the formula שִׁמְעוּ־נָא (listen! now!). Furthermore, I regard 3:8 as part of the section 3:1–8, because, as I will argue later, the prophet is contrasting himself with the leadership in his society. Micah 3:1–8 may be further subdivided into verses 1–4 and 5–8, and 3:9–12 into 9–10 and 11–12.[11] Verse 5 starts with the typical prophetic formula כֹּה אָמַר יהוה (this says Yahweh). The more general approach is to regard 3:1–4; 3:5–8 and 3:9–12 as three judgement proclamations by the prophet.

Ethics, (ed. Robin Gill; Cambridge: Cambridge University Press, 2001), 195–208; Christopher J. H. Wright, *Old Testament Ethics for the People of God* (Leicester, UK: InterVarsity, 2004).

John Rogerson, "Old Testament and Christian Ethics" (*Cambridge Companion to Christian Ethics*, 9–41) alerts readers to the problems when using the biblical text (in this regard the OT) for ethical guidance, but indicates also the positives it can contribute to the debate on ethics and the Bible.

7. Walter Brueggemann, "Next steps in Jeremiah studies?," in *Troubling Jeremiah* (ed. A. R. Pete Diamond, Kathleen M. O'Connor, and Louis Stulman; JSOTSup 260; Sheffield: Sheffield Academic Press, 1999), 404–22 (412).

8. Johanna Stiebert, *The Exile and the Prophet's Wife: Historical Events and Marginal Perspectives* (Interfaces Series; Collegeville, Minn.: Liturgical, 2005), 68.

9. Cf. Robert P. Carroll, "The Book of Jeremiah: Intertextuality and Ideological Criticism," in *Troubling Jeremiah*, 220–43; also Stiebert, *Exile and the Prophet's Wife*, 65–69.

10. Charles S. Shaw, *The Speeches of Micah: A Rhetorical-historical Analysis* (JSOTSup 145; Sheffield: JSOT Press, 1993), 101.

11. Jan A Wagenaar, *Judgment and Salvation: The Composition and Redaction of Micah 2–5* (VTSup 85; Leiden: Brill, 2001), 242.

Utzschneider, however, differs with this view.¹² He approaches the Micah text as a prophetic drama, consisting of different acts and scenes. Micah 3 in his view would form part of the second scene of act two (2:6—4:7) of the Micah drama. This second scene has two parts, namely 3:1-8 and 3:9-12.¹³ In Micah 3:1-8, Utzschneider says: "Die Lexis dieses Auftritts is dominiert durch die Ich-Reden, die ihn einfassen (V. 1, erster Satz / V. 8) und die zweimal neu einsetzen (V. 3 und 5: mein Volk)."¹⁴ Of 3:9-12, he observes that "Die Lexis des Abschnitts, der am ehesten dem Gattungsschema des prophetischen Gerichtswortes entspricht, ist durch die direkte Anrede an die 'Häupter und Vorsteher' bestimmt."¹⁵ In the first part of this scene (3:1-8) the focus is on a "silent God," whereas 3:9-12 depicts a "Godless" Zion. From the point of interest in power and leadership, which is the focus of the present study, both of these themes that Utzschneider suggests (Yahweh's silence and Zion without Yahweh) are the result of a failing leadership. These leaders had positions of power in their society, but they have abused the power these positions grant them.

Micah 3:1-8

The first subsection consists of Micah 3:1-4.

(3:1) ואמר שמעו־נא ראשי יעקב וקציני בית ישראל

(3:2) הלוא לכם לדעת את המשפט: שנאי טוב ואהבי רעה
גזלי עורם מעליהם ושארם מעל עצמותם.

(3:3) ואשר אכלו שאר עמי ועורם מעליהם
הפשיטו ואת עצמתיהם פצחו ופרשו כאשר

(3:4) בסיר וכבשר בתוך קלחת: אז יזעקו אל יהוה
ולא יענה אותם ויסתר פניו מהם בעת
ההיא כאשר הרעי מעלליהם

---

12. Helmut Utzschneider, *Michas Reise in die Zeit. Studien zum Drama als Genre der prophetischen Literatur des Alten Testaments.* (Stuttgarter Bibelstudien 180; Stuttgart: Katholischer Bibelwerk, 1999).

13. Mignon R Jacobs, *The Conceptual Coherence of the Book of Micah* (JSOTSup 322; Sheffield: Sheffield Academic Press, 2001), 86-89, also suggests a two-fold division, but for different reasons than Utzschneider. He substantiates his division on "... first the generic features and second the conceptual signals" of chapter 3. In 3:1-8 the focus is on the sin of the leaders and in 3:9-12, although the leaders are also involved, the entire city Zion is the focus of judgment.

14. Utzschneider, *Michas Reise*, 139.

15. Ibid., 146.

Then I said, "Listen, you leaders of Jacob, you rulers of the house of Israel. Should you not know justice (מִשְׁפָּט)?, (2) you who hate good and love evil; who tear the skin from my people and the flesh from their bones; (3) who eat my people's flesh, strip off their skin and break their bones in pieces; who chop them up like meat for the pan, like flesh for the pot?" (4) Then, they will cry out to the LORD, but he will not answer them. At that time he will hide his face from them because of the evil they have done. (NIV)

The introduction of verse 1, referring to a first person singular (וָאֹמַר, here "Then I said"), has created many debates over time. The Septuagint has it as a third person masculine singular perfect, but Hagstrom regards this reading as unlikely.[16] Up to date there is still no consensus on the issue.[17] In the light of the nature of the text in chapter 2, it seems that chapter 3 continues the dialogue between the prophet Micah and some adversaries. Jacobs regards chapter 3 as a response to 2:6–11.[18] I take the first person as referring to the prophet as the representative of Yahweh, addressing the leadership in Judah. The same applies to the first person singular in 3:8.

In verse 1 of this passage Micah is addressing the secular leadership, referring to them as leaders and rulers. "Rulers" probably refers to heads of families or clans. Because the terms are used in parallel, this is probably a general reference to political and community leadership, including civilian and military leaders.[19] The prophet addresses himself to these leaders because they show no respect for righteousness and justice and because, figuratively, they devour their own people like cannibals.

The subsection 3:1–4 clearly rebukes political leaders for their insensitivity to what is right. They are the ones primarily responsible for ensuring that justice prevails. The leaders are accused of loving injustice and hating what is good. Because of this, Yahweh will not hear them when they call.

---

16. David Gerald Hagstrom, *The Coherence of the Book of Micah: A Literary Analysis* (SBLDS 89; Atlanta, Ga.: Scholars Press, 1988), 138.

17. Cf. Charles S. Shaw, *The Speeches of Micah: A Rhetorical-Historical Analysis* (JSOTSup 145; Sheffield: JSOT Press, 1993), 97; Bruce K. Waltke, *A Commentary on Micah* (Grand Rapids, Mich.: Eerdmans, 2007), 144–46; also Utzschneider, *Michas Reise*, 128–29.

18. Jacobs, *Conceptual Coherence*, 84–85; also in the regard, cf. A. S. Van der Woude, *Micha: Die Prediking van het Oude Testament* (De Prediking van het Oude Testament; Kampen: Kok, 1976), 10–11, 61–64.

19. Cf. N. A. Schuman, *Micha: verklaring van een Bijbelgedeelte* (Kampen: Kok, 1989), 61; Juan I. Alfaro, *Justice and Loyalty: A Commentary on the Book of Micah* (ITC; Grand Rapids, Mich.: Eerdmans, 1989), 33.

Micah 3:5–8

The second subsection is formed by Micah 3:5–8.

(3:5) כה אמר יהוה על הנביאים המתעים את עמי
הנשכים בשניהם וקראו שלום ואשר לא יתן על פיהם
(3:6) וקדשו עליו מלחמה: לכן לילה לכם מחזון וחשכה
לכם מקסם ובאה השמש על הנביאים וקדר עליהם היום:
(3:7) ובשו החזים וחפרו הקסמים ועטו על שפם כלם
(3:8) כי אין מענה אלהים: ואולם אנכי מלאתי כח
את־רוח יהוה ומשפט וגבורה להגיד ליעקב פשעו ולישראל חטאתו

> Thus says the LORD concerning the prophets who lead my people astray, who cry "Peace" when they have something to eat, but declare war against those who put nothing into their mouths. (6) Therefore it shall be night to you, without vision, and darkness to you, without revelation. The sun shall go down upon the prophets, and the day shall be black over them; (7) the seers shall be disgraced, and the diviners put to shame; they shall all cover their lips, for there is no answer from God. (8) But as for me, I am filled with power (כֹּחַ), with the Spirit of the LORD (אֶת־רוּחַ יהוה), and with justice (מִשְׁפָּט) and might (גְּבוּרָה), to declare to Jacob his transgression and to Israel his sin." (NRSV)

In 3:5–8 the focus shifts to religious leaders. The first of these are the prophets (v. 5), who are accused of proclaiming peace to those who do them favours but make war on those who do not submit to their claims. They will be punished by losing their ability to reveal the unknowable—the very power for which they are esteemed. Without the God-given knowledge to which they lay claim, ". . . therefore it shall be night to you, without vision, and darkness to you, without revelation. The sun shall go down upon the prophets, and the day shall be black over them" (3:6). All that gives meaning to their existence will be nullified. Micah 3:6–7 lists other categories of religious functionaries (seers, diviners, soothsayers), all of whom generally claim to have insights into the divine that are denied to ordinary people. Grabbe has made a detailed study of all these personages and their functions.[20] It would appear that some of the older religious figures continued to function alongside the prophets who

---

20. Lester L. Grabbe, *Priests, Prophets, Diviners, Sages: A Socio-Historical Study of Religious Specialists in Ancient Israel* (Valley Forge, Pa.: Trinity Press International, 1995).

formed part of the prophetic tradition in Israel en Judah.[21] Micah lists them all in the same breath. According to him, they too—like the political leaders—will be shamed: Yahweh will not hear them either (cf. vs. 4, 6, 7).

Micah 3:8

The focus of the present study is Micah 3:8:

ואולם אנכי מלאתי כח את־רוח יהוה ומשפט וגבורה
להגיד ליעקב פשעו ולישראל חטאתו

But as for me, I am filled (מָלֵאתִי) with power (כֹּחַ), with the Spirit of the LORD (אֶת־רוּחַ יהוה), and with justice (מִשְׁפָּט) and might (גְּבוּרָה), to declare to Jacob his transgression and to Israel his sin.

There is no doubt whatsoever that this verse is part of 3:5–8. It contrasts Micah with the spiritual leaders mentioned in 3:5–7. Andersen and Freedman consider it to be a personal utterance of Micah's: ". . . an *apologia* for the forthrightness of the oracles in which it is embedded."[22] If this is taken to mean that it is a kind of apology for the harshness of his words, it presents the prophet as somewhat unsure of himself; but the opposite is in fact the case. It seems, rather, that Micah is emphasising the authority with which he speaks, an authority derived directly from Yahweh. I prefer to align myself with Simundson,[23] who sees it as part of a "call narrative" which is not given in full. It is the first person singular that chiefly indicates the prophet's intention of stressing his calling.

Much has been written about the grammar of 3:8. The phrase אֶת־רוּחַ יהוה (with the Spirit of Yahweh) in particular may appear to disturb the balance of the verse. McKane lists a good many possibilities proposed by researchers to resolve this problem.[24] The easiest would be, of course, to omit the phrase as a later addition.[25]

---

21. Cf. Daniel J. Simundson, *Hosea, Joel, Amos, Obadiah, Jonah, Micah* (AOTC; Nashville, Tenn.: Abingdon, 2005), 315.

22. Francis I. Andersen and David Noel Freedman, *Micah: A New Translation with Introduction and Commentary* (AB 24E; New York: Doubleday, 2000), 376.

23. Simundson, *Hosea, Joel, Amos, Obadiah, Jonah, Micah*, 312, 316.

24. William McKane, *The Book of Micah: Introduction and Commentary* (Edinburgh: T&T Clark, 1998), 108–109.

25. Cf. McKane, *Book of Micah*, 110; Wilhelm Rudolph, *Micha, Nahum, Habakuk, Zephanja: Mit einer Zeittafel von Alfred Jepson* (KAT 13/3; Gütersloh: Gerd Mohn, 1975), 68; Wagenaar, *Judgment and*

Wolff follows Wellhausen who regards the mentioned phrase as a later commentary added to the text. He substantiates his view by reasoning that the phrase "interrupts the three-stress colon (authority—justice—courage)" and thereby "overloads the prosody of the unit;" and furthermore "it adds a superfluous אֵת."[26]

However, I am more comfortable with the judgment of Andersen and Freedman[27] that the phrase should be left in. The *nota accusativi* אֶת־רוּחַ יהוה (with the Spirit of Yahweh) is probably the object of the verb "fill." Micah is filled with the Spirit of Yahweh, and this is associated with three nouns: כֹּחַ (power), מִשְׁפָּט (justice) and גְּבוּרָה (might). Waltke agrees that there is a problem with the grammar.[28] Nevertheless, the argument that the phrase אֶת־רוּחַ יהוה disturbs the rhythm of the verse seems to him inadequate; he thinks that we know too little about verse rhythm. In his estimation, "... the accusative: כֹּחַ (power), complements יְמַלֵּא (filled) which is linked with רוּחַ (Spirit) . . . ."[29] He goes on to say that מִשְׁפָּט (justice) and גְּבוּרָה (might) too, are accusatives complementing the verb מָלֵאתִי. According to Andersen and Freedman,[30] the latter two nouns are "in delayed coordination with כֹּחַ (power).

Be that as it may, כֹּחַ (power) is associated with the Spirit of Yahweh (יהוה רוּחַ). I am particularly intrigued by the association of כֹּחַ (power) with the prophetic ministry. As far as I have been able to confirm, this is the only time the concept כֹּחַ (power) in conjunction with the verb מָלֵא (fill) is applied to a prophet. Prophets are often associated with the Spirit of Yahweh (רוּחַ יהוה); see 1 Sam 10:6; 1 Kgs 18:12; 22:21f; 2 Kgs 2:9, 16; also Isa 61:1). As far as the Minor Prophets are concerned, this qualification of Micah's ministry reminds one of Hosea 9:7-8. In this passage the prophet is referred to as a אִישׁ הָרוּחַ (man of the inspiration). According to Wolff this description demonstrates Hosea's ability to speak. He argues that "... hier ist der Geist vor allem die 'Triebkraft zum Reden.'"[31] This is also true of the prophet Micah.

Salvation, 246–47, among others.

26. Hans Walter Wolff, *Micah: A Commentary* (trans. Gary Stansell; CC; Minneapolis, Minn.: Augsburg, 1990), 91–92.

27. Andersen and Freedman, *Micah*, 377.

28. Waltke, *Commentary on Micah*, 166.

29. Ibid.

30. Andersen and Freedman, *Micah*, 377.

31. Hans Walter Wolff, *Dodekapropheten 1. Hosea* (Neukirchen Kreis Moers: Neukirchener Verlag, 1961), 202.

In the light of this association of Micah with the prophet Hosea, it would seem that Micah continued in the Israelite prophetic tradition of which Hosea was also part.

However, as indicated, the correlation of Micah's prophetic ministry with power seems quite unique. According to Waltke, the term should be translated as "energy" or "vigour."[32] He refers to Renaud, who considers the term כֹּחַ to express the dynamic of prophetic performance. I am inclined to agree with the interpretation proposed by Wolff that, "כֹּחַ means both physical and psychic strength, also to endure in opposition and discouragement."[33] Besides power (כֹּחַ), Micah 3:8 indicates that the prophet is endowed with מִשְׁפָּט (justice) and גְּבוּרָה (might). Kessler rightly notes in this regard, "Mit >>Kraft... und Recht und Stärke<< werden Micha Eigenschaften zugesprochen, die wohl jedem Menschen zukommen können, wie man sie aber besonders von Personen erwartet, die mit Autorität ausgestattet sind und Führungsaufgaben haben."[34] This implies that Yahweh has equipped Micah very well for the unpopular task he had to perform in his confrontation with the leadership in his society.

It is not, however, a sound practice to transfer a word's meaning into a different context. The context in which it is used must help to determine its meaning. It may of course be that Micah needed physical strength and energy on account of the opposition he experienced from other prophets, but to me the key to an understanding of the word lies in the contrast verse 8 presents to the spiritual leaders mentioned in verses 5–7. Researchers agree that the function of verse 8 is to express the contrast between Micah and his opponents.[35] If we look at it in this light, the meaning of כֹּחַ (power) must be sought in a contrast to the powerlessness of the opposing spiritual leaders. To me, כֹּחַ (power) signifies that Micah, by contrast with that "powerlessness," has been empowered by Yahweh. That is what the Spirit of Yahweh (יהוה רוּחַ) does for him. He is filled with the empowering Spirit (רוּחַ). The empowering Spirit of Yahweh confers on Micah everything the opposing religious leader's lack, all that had made them credible religious authorities in the first place, such as revelations, special knowledge, and insight into the future. They have lost these abilities. Micah, on the other hand, now has what they have lost: the attributes of רוּחַ, which

---

32. Waltke, *Commentary on Micah*, 166.

33. Hans Walter Wolff, *Micah the Prophet* (trans. Ralph D. Gehrke; Philadelphia, Pa.: Fortress, 1981), 73.

34. Rainer Kessler, *Micha* (HThKAT; Freiburg: Herder, 22000), 157.

35. Andersen and Freedman, *Micah*, 376; Simundson, *Hosea, Joel, Amos, Obadiah, Jonah, Micah*, 316; McKane, *Book of Micah*, 108, among others.

include the ability to function as a true prophet. This involves insight and sensitivity as to what is right and to the advantage of people in society; also the daring and perseverance that make it possible to address leaders and point out the injustice of their actions. Yahweh has taken away the abilities of the other religious leaders who hate good and love evil (3:2); Micah, on the other hand, he has equipped by his רוּחַ (Spirit) with everything a true prophet needs for a credible ministry to the glory of Yahweh.

Micah 3:9–12

(3:9) שמעו־נא זאת ראשי בית יעקב וקציני בית ישראל
המתעבים משפט ואת כל הישרה יעקשו:
(3:10) בנה ציון בדמים וירושלם בעולה:
(3:11) ראשיה בשחד ישפטו וכהניה במחיר יורו ונביאיה בכסף יקסמו ועל יהוה ישענו לאמר הלוא יהוה בקרבנו לא תבוא
(3:12) עלינו רעה: לכן בגללכם ציון שדה תחרש וירושלם עיין תהיה והר הבית לבמות יער

> Hear this, you leaders of house of Jacob, you rulers of the house of Israel, who despise justice (מִשְׁפָּט) and distort all that is right; (10) who build Zion with bloodshed, and Jerusalem with wickedness. (11) Her leaders judge for a bribe, her priests teach for a price, and her prophets tell fortunes for money. They lean upon the LORD and say, "Is not the LORD among us? No disaster will come upon us." (12) Therefore because of you, Zion will be ploughed like a field, Jerusalem will become a heap of rubble, the temple hill a mound overgrown with thickets. (NIV)

Once again, in verse 9, the political leaders are called upon to listen. Once again they are accused of injustice. They harm people, they do violence. They are told that they built Jerusalem with the blood of their people. Forced labour has cost lives (v. 10). Verse 11 further portrays injustice in the city in terms of lawyers who take bribes and priests who demand payment for their revelations. Prophets, too, demand pay. They go even further: they presume to claim that Yahweh is with them. Verse 12 concludes the passage with a judgment. Because the state of affairs has become so terrible, Yahweh will punish these leaders. He will destroy Jerusalem (Zion) and the temple heights will be overgrown and inaccessible. The symbols of Yahweh's presence (the city and temple) will be no more. Verses 3:1–8 stated that Yahweh would cut off communication with them; the subsequent passage 3:9–12 goes even further—Yahweh will withdraw from them and he will destroy Jerusalem (Zion). Micah 3:1–12 is a judgment on the leaders and it has consequences for the people of Judah.

I have argued, in an article about this pericope, that there is a link between the שָׁלוֹם (peace) spoken of in 3:5 and the excessive confidence of the leaders that Yahweh is with them despite their injustice and evil. All the elements of the Royal/temple-Zion ideology are involved. The king on the throne, the temple in the city of Zion, the assurance of Yahweh's unconditional presence in their midst—all this brings about a mistaken confidence in the theology (ideology) to which they cling so blindly.[36] It creates a false sense of peace and security.

Micah 3:8 and the Debate about Power

Micah can probably be read at different levels. I delineate two of them as follows. First, if one reconstructs Micah as a prophet from Moresheth-Gath, this makes for an interesting reading of 3:8. According to this, Micah would be the representative of a rural "constitution,"[37] who had come to Jerusalem to protect the interests of rural people. Other scholars have suggested that he might have been the representative of an organised group working for better social conditions for the people, especially those in rural areas.[38] So, Micah comes to Jerusalem to expose the abuses of power practised by the leadership. He establishes his power in terms of verse 3:8, basing his claim on the authority of Yahweh. Waltke sees the social context wherein Micah's performance is ". . . endowed with a strength and courage from God that does not flinch from the lonely role of standing against the entire power structure in Jerusalem."[39] In terms of "performance," 3:8 would have been particularly impressive. It would have had a potent effect on the audience and on his opponents (who were

---

36. Wilhelm J. Wessels, "Wisdom in the gate: Micah takes the rostrum," *OTE* 10/1 (1997): 125–35 (131).

37. Cf. Wolff, *Micah the Prophet*, 17–25; Frank S. Frick, *A Journey through Hebrew Scriptures* (Belmont, Calif.: Wadsworth/Thompson, 22003), 370; Joseph Blenkinsopp, *Sage, Priest, Prophet: Religious and Intellectual Leadership in Ancient Israel* (Library of Ancient Israel; Louisville, Ky.: Westminster/John Knox, 1995), 154.

38. Delbert R. Hillers, *Micah: A Commentary on the Book of the Prophet Micah* (ed. Paul D. Hanson with Loren Fisher; Hermeneia; Philadelphia, Pa.: Fortress, 1984), 4.

39. Waltke, *Commentary on Micah*, 174.

cut off from Yahweh). In this way the Spirit of Yahweh would confirm his power as against the powerlessness of his opponents.

Second, a reading of Micah 3:8 in the literary context of the pericope and of the book as a whole brings out a somewhat different focus. The broader issue in the book, which Micah exemplifies, is the question of true and false prophets and therefore of false prophecy. As early as chapter 2, conflict is already building between Micah and the other prophets.[40] The latter support the Jerusalem leadership, thereby earning esteem and a form of power among the people of Judah and Jerusalem.[41] They proclaim salvation, making positive prophecies which obviously make them popular with both people and leadership. In 3:8, on the other hand, Micah emerges as a true prophet by not hesitating to prophesy doom as the punishment of unrighteousness. He is able to do this because the Spirit of Yahweh empowers him.[42] Because he has established his position of power through his connection with Yahweh, he seizes the opportunity: he exposes the social injustice of the Jerusalem leadership and their supporters like the true prophet he is.

When the text is read in this way, it means that the prophet's words were used by others (editors) to create a written text. As Doan and Gilles have shown, it is no longer a question of the prophetic performance through which the prophet influenced his audience. The literary text exercises its own power on the readers or hearers of the text.[43] It is something new, because the editors have given a new context to the prophetic words. The text of Micah is a collection of pronouncements arranged according to a chosen pattern for a particular purpose. To my way of thinking, this purpose had to do with the question of true or false prophets. In chapter 3 of the Micah text, and particularly in 3:8, it is clearly stated that the Spirit of Yahweh must be the source of empowerment. This confers the "power base" from which the prophet speaks. The Spirit also confers the courage not to flinch from exposing un-

---

40. Van der Woude, *Micha*, 10–11; Wessels, "Conflicting Powers," 531–34.

41. Waltke, *Commentary on Micah*, 2.

42. J. P. Van der Westhuizen, "The Holy Spirit in the Old Testament," in *The reality of the Holy Spirit in the Church. FS F. P. Möller* (ed. Petrus J. Gräbe and Willem J. Hattiingh; Pretoria: Van Schaik, 1997), 42–52 (48), regards the power connected with the Spirit of Yahweh in Micah 3:8 as "mental or spiritual power executing *justice* and *authority* (might)." For a broader discussion of the Spirit of Yahweh in the OT, cf. M. J. H. van Niekerk, "The Spirit of God in the Old Testament," in *Reality of the Holy Spirit in the Church*, 27–41, and also the study of Christopher J. H. Wright, *Knowing the Holy Spirit through the Old Testament* (Downers Grove, Ill.: InterVarsity, 2006).

43. Doan and Giles, *Prophets, Performance and Power*, passim.

righteousness. A true prophet is on the side of righteousness. The editors represent Micah to be such a prophet.

In terms of the general discussion about power, Micah acts from a position of power as a true prophet. According to 3:8, his empowerment by the Spirit of Yahweh gives him the right to such a position. Also by virtue of his empowerment, he displays a sound judgment about right and wrong and can therefore state his case with the strength of conviction.

The contrast between Micah 3:8 on the one hand and 3:1–4 and 3:5–7 on the other also points to an abuse of power. Power and righteousness must go hand in hand if power is not to result in abuse. Wolff quotes Pascal: "Justice without power is powerless. Power without justice is tyrannical. . . . Justice and power must therefore be connected so that what is just is also powerful and what is powerful just."[44] This is precisely what happened in the society Micah lived in. Leaders became obsessed with power and sought support for their conduct, but power and justice had become separated. The criterion for good leadership in Israel and Judah was the context of a covenant bond with Yahweh. It implied an obligation to ensure that justice was done and people's rights protected. The king in particular was charged with justice to disempowered people such as widows and orphans: their rights to such things as land ownership and a free and peaceful way of life. But in the society Micah lived in, this did not happen. Prophets and priests were supposed to ensure that leaders did their duty in these matters; but because they wanted the goodwill of the leaders, they pretended blindness to injustice. Worse, they concocted religious justifications for the conduct of kings and leaders. This is a good example of how leaders (in this context, political leaders) expanded their power base by canvassing the support of influential people such as religious leaders. It enabled them to establish their influence on a broad basis in society.

The religious leaders gave religious support to an idea, making it a power idea or ideology by means of which ordinary citizens could be dominated. They promoted a false understanding of the Royal/temple-Zion ideology by neglecting to expose the injustice of exploiting and ill-treating people. They strengthened the hands of bad political leaders by keeping silent about the conditionality of Yahweh's presence with Judah: namely, that Yahweh, in his relationship with Judah, had set ethical requirements. The religious leaders went even further by exploiting for their own advantage the unjust system established by the political leaders. Both political and religious

---

44. Wolff, *Micah the Prophet*, 151–52.

leaders had lapsed into an abuse of their power. Dempsey gives a brief but excellent summary of power abuse by the Judean leaders.[45]

Conclusion

From the discussion it should be clear that there is a definite relation between people in positions of leadership and power. Without exercising some form of power, leadership will fail. Governmental positions in societies are generally regarded as positions with some degree of power. This is also true of the Israelite and Judean societies. When it comes to leadership positions in other spheres of the life such as the religious one, power is not by default associated with these positions. However, it is clear that priests, prophets and other religious figures had power due to their claimed divine connections. People also empowered them by recognising their supernatural abilities. Because they held these positions in their respective societies, they had to account for the ways in which they exercised their power. The case study in Micah 3:8 has illustrated how a prophet defines his ministry in terms of power.

This study has also shown that the leadership in Judah, civil and religious have abused their power. The book of Micah contains a clear portrayal of power abuse; but it is not only about power but also about powerlessness. Chapters 2 and 3 spell out how powerful leaders abused their power to the detriment of powerless people; and chapter 3 also shows how, on the other hand, religious functionaries (prophets, priests, seers, diviners) who had lost the favour of Yahweh were powerless against a prophet empowered by the Spirit of Yahweh to exercise a forceful prophetic ministry (3:8). Then, too, power must remain within ethical bounds if it is not to degenerate into power abuse. Micah clearly states that leaders have to exercise their power to promote justice and righteousness or it would be regarded as a failed leadership. Power correctly exercised will benefit people in societies.

---

45. Carol J. Dempsey, *The Prophets: A Liberation-Critical Reading* (Minneapolis, Minn.: Fortress, 2000), 28–31.

The Narrative and Rhetorical Use of Divine Necessity in Luke-Acts

KENNETH BASS

Kenneth_Bass@baylor.edu
Baylor University, Waco, Texas 76798

Introduction

In recent years, rhetorical criticism has received a hearing in NT studies. Several important works have been offered on the subject in the last twenty-five years.[1] In addition, two recent collections of essays offer continuing guidance to those who wish to sharpen their rhetorical critical skills.[2] By now, it should be apparent that those who want to take the NT seriously will have to recognize the role of rhetorical criticism. Only recently, however, have NT scholars begun to consider rhetorical education in the Greco-Roman world as represented by the rhetorical handbooks and the *progymnasmata*,[3] the latter serving as exercises for students participating in

---

1. George Kennedy, *New Testament Interpretation through Rhetorical Criticism* (Chapel Hill, N.C.: University of North Carolina Press, 1984); Vernon Robbins, *Jesus the Teacher: A Socio-Rhetorical Interpretation of Mark* (Philadelphia, Pa.: Fortress, 1984); idem, *The Tapestry of Early Christian Discourse: Rhetoric, Society, and Ideology* (New York, N.Y.: Routledge, 1996); Burton Mack, *Rhetoric and the New Testament* (Philadelphia, Pa.: Fortress, 1990); Margret Mitchell, *Paul and the Rhetoric of Reconciliation* (Louisville, Ky.: Westminster John Knox, 1991); Mark D. Given, *Paul's True Rhetoric* (Emory Studies in Early Christianity; ed. Vernon K. Robbins; Harrisburg, Pa.: Trinity International, 2001); Clare Rothschild, *Luke-Acts and the Rhetoric of History* (WUNT 2/175; Tübingen: Mohr Siebeck, 2004).

2. *Handbook of Classical Rhetoric in the Hellenistic Period: 330 B.C. – A.D. 400* (ed. Stanley Porter; Leiden: Brill, 1997); *Contextualizing Acts: Lukan Narrative and Greco-Roman Discourse* (ed. Todd Penner and Caroline Vander Stichele; SBLSymS 20; Atlanta, Ga.: Society of Biblical Literature, 2003), with a review by Paul Elbert in *RBL*, http://www.bookreviews.org/pdf/4026_5045.pdf.

3. E.g., respectively, Cicero, *Rhetorica Ad Herennium* (LCL 403; Cambridge, Mass.: Harvard University Press, 1999), and George Kennedy, *Progymnasmata: Greek Textbooks of Prose Composition and Rhetoric* (SBLWGRW 10; Atlanta, Ga.: Society of Biblical Literature, 2003).

the rhetorical curriculum. Especially important as a contemporary of Luke are the *progymnasmata* of Aelius Theon.[4]

This study will argue that an examination of Luke's rhetorical use of necessity can be aided by understanding the role of necessity in Aelius Theon's *progymnasmata*, especially the section dealing with narrative. First, I will offer a review of recent scholarship on divine necessity in Luke-Acts. Second, I will introduce the *progymnasmata*, and argue for a reading of Luke-Acts that takes that rhetorical tradition into consideration. Third, an analysis of δεῖ in Luke-Acts will be offered. Finally, I will bring the conclusions of the previous three sections together in an investigation of Luke's rhetorical strategy regarding divine necessity. Examples will come from Luke 9:22 (Jesus' prediction of his suffering, rejection, death, and resurrections); Acts 1:16–21 (the replacement of Judas); and from Acts 19:21; 23:11; and 27:24 (the necessity of Paul's visit to Rome), followed by some concluding observations and comments.

Survey of Scholarship

NT scholars have examined the providence of God, especially divine necessity, in Luke-Acts with varying results. Henry Cadbury was well aware of divine guidance in Luke-Acts:

> The divine intervention is one of the credentials of the Christian movement. Possibly this thought is already in [Luke's] mind when he speaks of his subject as "the things *fulfilled* among us." Like others he was sensitive to the detailed fulfillments of Scripture, but his references to this trait of Christianity are more general than in the other evangelists and convey a slightly different meaning.[5]

Cadbury also noted that Luke used the Scripture more apologetically than Matthew; often the Scripture in Luke is associated with a situation that is difficult to believe, such as the death, burial, resurrection, and ascension of Jesus.

---

4. The latest critical edition is Michael Patillon, *Aelius Théon Progymnasmata: Texte établi et traduit* (Avec l'assistance, pour l'Arménien, de Giancarlo Bolognesi; Collection des Universités de France: Paris: Société d'édition Les Belles Lettres, 1997).

5. Henry J. Cadbury, *The Making of Luke-Acts* (Peabody, Mass.: Hendrickson, [2]1999), 303–4 (emphasis his).

Walter Grundmann notes that the idea of divine providence behind δεῖ is present in the Greek literature.[6] However, this divine providence is related more closely to the idea of fate, thus the choice of an *impersonal* auxiliary. A tension exists between the Greek idea of fate and the OT idea of the providence of a personal, caring God. Grundmann writes,

> When the LXX, the Hellenistic Jews and even more so the NT adopt the word, they speak a language understood by those whom they are attempting to reach. And by linking it with, and referring it to, the biblical view of God, they make it plain that it no longer expresses the neutral necessity of fate. Instead, it indicates the will of God declared in the message. This is the standpoint from which it is applied in many different ways.[7]

Following Cadbury and Grundmann, Erich Fascher[8] and Sigfried Schulz[9] produced studies on divine providence in Luke-Acts. Fascher basically followed Grundmann's notion that whereas the Greek idea of Fate was present in δεῖ, the NT use was influenced by the OT's personal God. Schulz concluded that the divine δεῖ was the prophetic entity through which God controls every minute detail of life.

Charles Cosgrove, in his survey of the function of δεῖ, has concluded that there are four aspects of divine necessity in Luke-Acts.[10] First, it points back to God's ancient plan and grounds the kerygma in divine sanction. Second, it is a summons to obedience. Third, it is God's guarantee of his plan. Finally, the logic of divine necessity involves a dramatic-comedic understanding of salvation history as a stage set time and again for divine intervention so that the spotlight of history continuously shines on God's saving miracle. Cosgrove has given us a significant insight into the function of divine necessity in Luke-Acts, but he does not utilize ancient rhetoric to make his case.

Clare Rothschild understands the divine δεῖ to function rhetorically in Luke-Acts by means of what is called "proof by prediction."[11] Her argument centers on the

---

6. Walter Grundmann, "δεῖ, δέον ἐστί," *TDNT* 2:21–25; idem, "ἀναγκάζω, ἀναγκαῖος, ἀνάγκη," *TDNT* 1:344–47.

7. Grundmann, "δεῖ, δέον ἐστί," 22.

8. Erich Fascher, "Theologische Beobachtungen zu δεῖ," in *Neutestamentliche Studien für Rudolf Bultmann zu seinem 70. Geburtstag* (ed. Walther Eltester; BZNW 21; Berlin: Töpelmann, 1954), 228–54.

9. Sigfried Schulz, "Gottes Vorsehung bei Lukas," *ZNW* 54 (1963): 104–16.

10. Charles H. Cosgrove, "The Divine ΔΕΙ in Luke-Acts," *NovT* 26/2 (1984): 168–90 (190).

11. Rothschild, *Luke-Acts and Rhetoric of History*, 212.

claim that Luke used necessity as support for the unbelievable claims that he was making: "For Luke-Acts . . . δεῖ construes unfamiliar and/or implausible events of the narrative—any events for which the historian wishes to strengthen causation—as fulfilled predictions."[12] This view will be challenged below. Even though she rightly understands Luke's history to be shaped by rhetoric, she does not relate Luke's work to the progymnasmata.

Mark Reasoner challenges a supposed "institutional history" approach to Luke-Acts, arguing instead that the theme of Luke-Acts is "divine necessity in history."[13] Surely, Reasoner is correct to note that divine necessity "directly nourishes the ἀσφάλεια, or certainty, that the implied author of Luke-Acts seeks to generate among the text's readers both in regard to what they had been taught (Luke 1:4) and in regard to their own lives."[14] However, as Cosgrove and Rothschild, Reasoner does not make use of the progymnasmata or the rhetorical handbook tradition.

These previous studies show that δεῖ in Luke-Acts often is associated with divine necessity understood as the fulfillment of God's plan. It will be the goal of the rest of the present study to demonstrate how Luke uses this divine necessity in his narrative.

Analysis of Δεῖ in Luke-Acts

Throughout the Lukan corpus, necessity plays an important role in the narrative. An examination of the auxiliary verb δεῖ (it is necessary)[15] demonstrates that this verb is used by Luke more than by any other NT writer (Matthew 8, Mark 6, Luke-Acts 40, John 10, Pauline corpus 24, General epistles 5, Revelation 7). Given that Luke has written about one fourth of the NT, it is significant that his usage of δεῖ accounts for forty percent of its usage in the NT.[16] This high percentage suggests that necessity is an important part of Luke's narrative strategy.

---

12. Ibid., 187.

13. Mark Reasoner, "The Theme of Acts: Institutional History or Divine Necessity in History?" *JBL* 118/4 (1999): 635–59 (659). The "institutional history" approach is advocated by Hubert Cancik and is critiqued in Elbert's review of *Contextualizing* (n. 2).

14. Ibid., 650.

15. A broader study would include other terms, such as μέλλω and ὀφείλω, as well as places where fulfillment of prophecy plays a role in the narrative.

16. This does not include the other words that suggest divine necessity.

When we take a closer look at how this auxiliary is used in Luke-Acts some very interesting things come to light. First, in the gospel, δεῖ is a "Jesus-word"; of the eighteen uses in Luke, fourteen are on the lips of Jesus.[17] The final use of the word in Luke 24:44, ὅτι δεῖ πληρωθῆναι πάντα τὰ γεγραμμένα ἐν τῷ νόμῳ Μωϋσέως καὶ τοῖς προφήταις καὶ ψαλμοῖς περὶ ἐμοῦ (that everything written about me in the law of Moses and the prophets and the psalms must be fulfilled)[18] is very similar to its first use in Acts 1:16, ἔδει πληρωθῆναι τὴ γραφὴν ἥν προεῖπεν τὸ πνεῦμα τὸ ἅγιον διὰ στόματος Δαυὶδ περὶ Ἰούδα (the scripture had to be fulfilled, which the Holy Spirit spoke beforehand by the mouth of David, concerning Judas). The things written about Jesus had to be fulfilled, and the things written about Judas had to be fulfilled.

Second, in several places in Luke-Acts δεῖ is used in conjunction with references to suffering. Twelve of the forty uses of δεῖ in Luke-Acts, or thirty percent, refer to suffering in some way.[19] The suffering is primarily Jesus', although Paul and the believers are also subjects.

Third, once Jesus ascends, although he makes appearances from time to time in the text, δεῖ becomes an apostolic word. The first five occurrences in Acts are spoken by Peter (Acts 1:16, 21; 3:21; 4:12; and 5:29), then Jesus makes his first post-ascension appearance in the text (9:6, 16) in order to instruct Paul and Ananias concerning what it is necessary for Paul to do and to suffer. Of the final eleven utterances of the word, eight are from Paul (Acts 19:21; 20:35; 24:19; 25:10; 26:9; 27:21; 27:24; and 27:26).

In Luke, the necessity of the suffering of Jesus is alluded to on six different occasions (9:22; 13:33; 17:25; 22:37; 24:7, 26, 44).[20] In his comments on 9:22, Howard Marshall notes, "The verb δεῖ expresses the divine purpose which 'must' be fulfilled in the career of Jesus... The parallel passages 18:31; 24:46; Mk 9:12; 14:21 indicate that for Luke and the early church this 'must' lay in the necessity to fulfill what was

---

17. Luke 2:49; 4:43; 9:22; 11:42; 12:12; 13:16; 13:33; 17:25; 18:1; 19:5; 21:9; 22:37; 24:26; and 24:44. Also, I believe a strong case could be made for the inclusion of 24:46, though the critical text denies it; the infinitive παθεῖν may be taken appositionally, however, thus removing the need for δεῖ.

18. English translations in this study are from the NRSV.

19. Luke 9:22; 13:33; 17:25; 22:37; 24:26, 44; Acts 1:16; 9:16; 14:22; 17:3; 25:24; 26:9.

20. Joel Green, *The Gospel of Luke* (NICNT; Grand Rapids, Mich.: Eerdmans, 1997), 156, writes, "Jesus' aligning himself first with Gods' aim comes to the fore especially through his use of the expression 'it is necessary'—employed regularly throughout Luke-Acts as an indicator of salvation historical necessity."

laid down in the Scriptures."[21] All of the final four uses of δεῖ in Luke are references by Jesus or the angels (24:7) to the fulfillment of the Scriptures and the words of Jesus about his death and resurrection. Luke's narrative use of necessity was perhaps informed by his rhetorical training.

The *Progymnasmata*

Education in the ancient world followed a distinct plan. According to Richard Burridge,

> Education concentrated on reading and writing, basic literature and mathematics, as well as physical education. Rhetoric appeared at the secondary level during the teens with rhetorical analysis of literature and practice of the preliminary exercises (προγυμνάσματα) as is seen in the handbooks, but full rhetorical training formed the bulk of higher education for future public speakers, lawyers, and politicians.[22]

Burridge, after noting that "it is unlikely that the Gospel writers and their audience would have had higher rhetorical training," also warns scholars to "be cautious about reading off a direct connection between their narrative biographical texts and the formal oratory of the law court or assembly."[23] In his conclusion, however, Burridge does admit that because of "his command of several different Greek styles and his composition of speeches, it is not unreasonable that [Luke] might have had some rhetorical training which emerges in his writing."[24]

On the other hand, Mikael Parsons claims that Luke "cut his rhetorical teeth" on the progymnasmatic tradition.[25] The *progymnasmata* formed the basic exercises that a student would repeat in order to gain rhetorical competency. George Kennedy notes that "The curriculum described in these works, featuring a series of set exercises of increasing difficulty, was the source of facility in written and oral expression for many persons and training for speech in public life."[26] It is Parsons' claim that these exercises "were probably intended to facilitate the transition from

---

21. I. Howard Marshall, *The Gospel of Luke* (NIGTC; Grand Rapids, Mich.: Eerdmans, 1978), 369.

22. Richard Burridge, "The Gospel and Acts," in *Handbook of Classical Rhetoric in the Hellenistic Period*, 507–32 (510).

23. Ibid.

24. Ibid., 530.

25. Mikeal Parsons, "Luke and the *Progymnasmata*," in *Contextualizing Acts* (n. 2), 43–63 (44).

26. Kennedy, *Progymnasmata*, viii.

grammar school to the more advanced study of rhetoric."[27] The rhetorical exercises in the *progymnasmata* included practice in constructing *chreia* (concise statements or actions), fables, narratives, *topoi* (statements amplifying good or bad things or something agreed), *ekphrases* (descriptions), *prosopopoeia* (speech-in-character or personifications), *syncreses* (comparisons), theses, and arguments concerning a law.

It may be expected, then, that Luke's writing will exhibit the influence from the preliminary exercise tradition.[28] It is hoped, as Parsons has projected, "that mining the comments on narrative in the *progymnasmata* might give exegetical assistance at other points in understanding the literary conventions employed elsewhere in the Lukan narratives."[29]

Our understanding of the narrative function of divine necessity in Luke-Acts can be strengthened by consulting the progymnasmata, especially *The Exercises of Aelius Theon*. Theon describes a narrative as "language descriptive of things that have happened or as though they had happened."[30] It is quite certain that Luke-Acts falls under this description. In many of the places in Luke-Acts where the auxiliary verb δεῖ is used, Luke is following a rhetorical strategy like that mentioned by Theon in his discussion of narrative in his progymnasmata. In other places, although δεῖ is not used, divine necessity is present. This study will focus on some instances where δεῖ is present, and will explore these Lukan rhetorical strategies.

Theon on Narrative

As noted above, in his discussion of narrative, Theon teaches that narrative (διήγημα) is an account of what happened or as though it had happened.[31] The role that narrative played in ancient composition should be considered here.

---

27. Parsons, "Luke and the *Progymnasmata*," 44.

28. Craig G. Gibson, "Learning Greek History in the Ancient Classroom: The Evidence of the Treatises on Progymnasmata," *CP* 99/2 (2004): 103–29 (126), finds that rhetorical training in the *progymnasmata* had a lasting impact on students that can be discerned in their later compositions.

29. Parsons, "Luke and the *Progymnasmata*," 56.

30. Aelius Theon 78.16–17 (Patillon, *Progymn.*, 38).

31. Theon then goes on to list the six elements of the διηγήσεως that I cite immediately below. These six elements constitute the complete narration (ἡ τελεία διήγησις, 78.23 [Patillon, *Progymn.*, 38]). Some development is reflected in later progymnasmatists, where διήγημα comes to mean the exercise of narrative, whereas διήγησις "is the usual technical term for a 'narration' as part of a speech" (Kennedy, *Progymn.*, 4). See also the progymnasmatic writings of Hermogones where "A narrative (*diêgêma*) differs from a narration (*diêgêsis*) as a piece of poetry (*poiêma*) differs from a poetical work (*poiêsis*)" (Kennedy, *Progymn.*, 75). Narration is a group of narratives strung together. For a slightly dif-

Imagine an author like Luke sitting down to write an account of the life of Jesus. The entire account will follow the same basic outline that many ancient biographies took: origin, birth, upbringing, deeds performed (often, but not necessarily, related to the virtue they demonstrate), achievements, manner of death, events after death, and (often) a comparison with some other great figure.[32] This entire account may be thought of as a biographical narration, made up of many narratives that take on different functions throughout the work. There may be a narrative about Jesus' birth or one about his death or about some great deed he performed and a lesson or point that may be drawn from it.

A narrative, then, may be written about any one of the elements or properties of the elements of a narration. According to Theon, the six elements of narration (Στοιχεῖα δὲ τῆς διηγήσεως) are *person, action, place, time, manner,* and *cause*.[33] Each of these elements has its distinct properties. For example, when discussing the *person*, topics of interest include origin, nature, education, disposition, age, fortune, etc. If writing about the *action*, it is appropriate to mention, among other things, whether it is great or small, easy or difficult, necessary or unnecessary, or advantageous or not advantageous.[34] Also relevant to the topic of the present study are the properties of the element *manner*. Theon instructs, "To manner belong unwillingly or willingly, and each of these is divided into three things: the unwilling into done by ignorance, accident, and necessity; the willing into whether something was done by force or secretly or by deceit."[35] These properties will be taken up in more detail a bit later.

A narration has three virtues: clarity, conciseness, and credibility.[36] Theon spends some time discussing which of the three virtues should be kept in mind in what situations. Of most importance is a narrative's credibility "for this is its most special feature."[37] The methods for achieving credibility in the narrative include 1) employing "styles that are natural for the speakers and suitable for the subjects and

---

ferent take on narrative and narration, see the comments of Nicolaus the Sophist (Kennedy, *Progymn.*, 136) and John of Sardis (Kennedy, *Progymn.*, 183).

32. Michael W. Martin, "Progymnasmatic Topic Lists: A Compositional Template for Luke and Other *Bioi*?" *NTS* 54 (2008): 18–41.

33. Aelius Theon 78.17–21 (Patillon, *Progymn.*, 38).

34. Aelius Theon 78.28–30 (Patillon, *Progymn.*, 39).

35. Aelius Theon 79.12–15 (Kennedy, *Progymn.* 29).

36. Aelius Theon 79.20–21 (Patillon, *Progymn.*, 40).

37. Aelius Theon 79.28–29 (Kennedy, *Progymn.*, 29).

the places and the occasion"[38]; 2) adding the *cause* of the thing to the narration; and 3) putting the incredible in believable terms. Theon goes through the example of the Thebans and Plataens conflict over the city of Platea. The events that Thucydides used and the manner in which he told them are all probable and credible. For example, it is certainly probable that the Thebans would want to seize the city of Platea in time of peace because they knew war was inevitable and wanted to get the upper hand. He says that it is credible that the Plateans, due to the darkness, could have mistakenly assumed that many more enemy soldiers had entered their city, and after they realized that there were many less than they initially thought, they recounted their surrender and attacked. The fact that they recounted their surrender and attacked their attackers is a response to the mistake they made under confusion of darkness. This seems credible to Theon.

The first element of a narration that is directly related to necessity is *action*.[39] One consideration of action is whether it is necessary or unnecessary. This language is echoed in the section on thesis, where Theon writes, "Now the most general headings of practical theses are supported by argument from what is necessary and what is noble and what is beneficial and what is pleasant, and refuted from the opposites."[40] Theon's list of the properties of *action* include necessary or unnecessary, great or small, advantageous or not advantageous, and easy or difficult. He gives two examples in his discussion of thesis: a practical thesis (whether a wise man will engage in politics) and a theoretical thesis (do the gods exercise providential care for the world). The list of topics to support the practical thesis contains claims that it is possible, in accordance with nature, easy, he is not the first to do so, appropriate, just, reverent, and necessary.[41] The argument uses necessity because "it is necessary for the city to have someone giving thought for its future, and especially a good person; for without this a city could not survive."[42] Support for the theoretical thesis is taken generally from the same topics. The argument for the necessity of believing that the gods exercise providential care for the world follows the line of reasoning that "it is

---

38. Aelius Theon 84.19–21 (Kennedy, *Progymn.*, 33).

39. Theon lists fate/fortune (τύχη) and moral choice (προαίρεσις) as two properties of the element *person*. Both of these terms are related to necessity by way of virtue in human character. I will have more to say about this in a forthcoming dissertation, in which I address necessity from an audience-oriented perspective, "The Rhetorical Function of Divine Necessity in Luke's *Bios* of Jesus."

40. Aelius Theon 121.21–23 (Kennedy, *Progymn.*, 56).

41. Aelius Theon 123.4–124.5 (Kennedy, *Progymn.*, 57–58). The property list from the element *action* in narration shows that one may also argue that an action is *unnecessary, unjust,* or *not easy*.

42. Aelius Theon 124.3–5 (Kennedy, *Progymn.*, 58).

necessary for providence to exist; for if someone removed providence from the god he would remove also the conception of him we have, by which we comprehend his very existence; for it is because of the god's concern for us that we have belief in his being."[43] The determination of necessity of *action* in a narration follows this same line of thinking: was it something that had to be done for a good reason? Because Theon listed, in addition to necessity, advantage, justice, and honor as properties of an *action*, Vernon Robbins is convinced that "actions in a narrative, according to Theon, produce deliberative, judicial, or epideictic rhetorical discourse."[44] Key properties of action for deliberative discourse might be necessary or unnecessary, advantageous or not advantageous, and possible or impossible. Those for judicial may be just or unjust, and those for epideictic—dangerous or not dangerous, easy or difficult, honorable or dishonorable.

The second element of narration directly related to necessity is the *manner* of action. The way in which an action is undertaken was important for judicial, deliberative, and epideictic discourse. It was important for judicial because a person's guilt or innocence may be determined thereby. If a person acted unintentionally due to ignorance, accident, or necessity, their behavior could be excused.[45] As with *action*, the language of *manner* is echoed elsewhere in Theon's writings and may help us understand its use here. In a passage in the section on *prosopopoeia* Theon writes, "Whenever we seek forgiveness we shall have starting points from the following: first, that the action was unintentional, either through ignorance or chance or necessity."[46] This claim parallels information that is repeated in passages on encomium and *syncresis*. In Theon's *progymnasmata*, when writing of *syncresis* (comparison) he instructs his readers that they should, when comparing persons, prefer "things that

---

43. Aelius Theon 127.5–9 (Kennedy, *Progymn.*, 60).

44. Vernon K. Robbins, "Narrative in Ancient Rhetoric and Rhetoric in Ancient Narrative" in *Society of Biblical Literature 1996 Seminar Papers* (SBLSP 35; Atlanta, Ga.: Scholars Press, 1996), 368–84 (372). For description of these rhetorical genres (deliberative, judicial, or epideictic), cf. David E. Aune, *The Westminster Dictionary of New Testament and Early Christian Literature and Rhetoric* (Louisville, Ky.: Westminster John Knox, 2003), 418–20.

45. Acts provides an example of something done due to ignorance in 3:13–18, especially vv. 17–18. Peter addresses a crowd that had gathered because of the healing of the lame man. After pointing out to them how they had rejected and killed Jesus, Peter states, "And now, friends, I know that you acted in ignorance, as did your rulers. In this way God fulfilled what he had foretold through all the prophets, that his Messiah would suffer." Thus, because "in this way God fulfilled what he had foretold," this thing done in ignorance also has a component of necessity in it.

46. Aelius Theon 117.25–28 (Kennedy, *Progymn.*, 49).

were done by choice rather than by necessity (ἀνάγκην) or chance."[47] Similarly, of encomium, Theon says that when dealing with external goods that have come to a person through no great deed of their own, the rhetor should show "that the subject used the advantage prudently and as he ought, not mindlessly—for goods that result from chance rather than moral choice are the least source of praise . . . ."[48] Ignorance, fate, chance, and necessity are in direct conflict with choice and intention. Choice and intention are the two critical elements in determining guilt and innocence and praise and blame.

Actions that a person was forced to undertake versus those freely chosen was a topic of discussion among the rhetoricians and philosophers in the ancient world. Aristotle raised the question (*Nicomachean Ethics* 2.4.30) in a statement about how a person performs virtuous acts: the act is virtuous "if the agent is in a certain condition when he acts, first if he acts knowingly, second if he acts from choice, and choice of these things for their own sake, and thirdly if he acts from a stable and unchangeable state of character." The author of *Rhetoric to Alexander* includes several references to intentional choice when discussing eulogistic speeches and accusation and defense.[49] Actions that are chosen are suitable for amplification; involuntary actions have as one line of defense that they were done out of necessity.

One might then expect a narration of the life of Jesus to contain anecdotes from his life and ministry. Vernon Robbins is convinced that each anecdote "exhibits the art of making a long story short. But when all are put together, they hold the key for making a short story long. More than this, anecdotes are a key resource for making a story persuasive. They contain the insights into life that move people to indict or acquit, to act in one way rather than another, and to censure one person and praise another."[50] For the active readers of Luke to be convinced, the material must be clear, concise, and, most of all, credible.

The Lukan Rhetorical Strategy

How might an investigation of some of the examples of divine necessity demonstrate Luke's rhetorical strategy? We might suspect that Luke, when constructing his narra-

---

47. Aelius Theon 113.14 (Patillon, *Progymn.*, 79).
48. Aelius Theon 111:15–19 (Patillon, *Progymn.*, 76).
49. *Rhetoric to Alexander* 1426a.1; 1427a.4.
50. Robbins, "Narrative in Ancient Rhetoric and Rhetoric in Ancient Narrative," 370.

tive, has practiced what he learned. An examination of some passages will be helpful at this point.

Necessity and the Credible: The Suffering of Jesus

In Luke's gospel, Jesus speaks to his disciples of his imminent suffering, death, and resurrection. The first account of this is in 9:22, just after Peter has confessed that Jesus is "The Christ of God," Jesus tells the disciples: δεῖ τὸν υἱὸν τοῦ ἀνθρώπου πολλὰ παθεῖν καὶ ἀποδοκιμασθῆναι ἀπὸ τῶν πρεσβυτέρων καὶ ἀρχιερέων καὶ γραμματέων καὶ ἀποκτανθῆναι καὶ τῇ τρίτῃ ἡμέρᾳ ἐγερθῆναι (The Son of man must suffer many things, and be rejected by the elders and the chief priests and scribes, and be killed, and on the third day be raised). The four infinitives here are complementary to δεῖ: παθεῖν, ἀποδοκιμασθῆναι, ἀποκτανθῆναι, and ἐγερθῆναι.[51] These four infinitives outline the will of God for Jesus.

Here, according to Rothschild's thesis, Luke is shoring up an unbelievable event with the rhetoric of necessity. She believes that Jesus' claim that he must suffer, be rejected, be killed, and after three days, be raised from the dead, is nothing short of unbelievable and needs the support of divine necessity. Yet, there is another way in which Luke can and does deal with difficult material.

Parsons provides an excellent example of Luke's ability to present a difficult, perhaps unbelievable situation without resorting to the kind of rhetorical necessity that Rothschild supposes.[52] Mark presents the story of the call of the four fishermen (Mark 1:16-20) as if the fishermen simply walked off with a total stranger. Luke "makes changes in the story to 'tell the unbelievable in a believable way.'"[53] In Luke's story the healing of Simon's mother-in-law precedes the call story, and the story is told in such a way that Simon in presented as being aware of the miracle. In Luke 5:1-11, Simon is not merely "welcoming a stranger on board, but acknowledging the holy man who had already healed a family member."[54] Because this option was open to Luke when narrating hard-to-believe events, when he does use "necessity" in the narrative, we should not think that he is merely hoping to shore up a weak

---

51. Heinz Schürman, *Das Lukasevangelium I, Kommentar zu Kap. 1, 1 – 9, 50* (HTKNT3/1; Leipzig: St. Benno/Freiburg: Herder, 1969), in his discussion of 9:22, stresses that the last of these infinitives, "enthüllt sich schon in dem göttlichen δεῖ (vlg 17, 25; 24, 7)" and that "Das Passiv ἐγερθῆναι entspricht dem verfügten δεῖ von V 22a" (533–39 [534, 535]).

52. Parsons, "Luke and the *Progymnasmata*," 56.

53. Ibid.

54. Ibid.

argument. Instead, he is using the property of "necessity" to establish an action in his narrative. Necessity for Luke means "part of the plan of God." Is Luke telling his audience that Jesus' death is necessary in some positive sense? Or is he pleading Jesus' case, arguing that Jesus did what he did out of necessity? How can a person's claim that he must suffer, die, and be resurrected be presented in a believable way?

If we apply the things we learned about narrative from Theon to the material leading up to Luke 9:22, we see that the Jesus who speaks of the necessity of his suffering has just been declared to be the Christ of God. Not only this, but as has been clear from the beginning of the work, this Jesus is no ordinary individual. Charles Talbert has noted the significance of the opening section of Luke (1:1–4:15) for understanding the character of Jesus. In reference to the genre of "an account of the pre-public career of a great person," he writes,

> The genre functioned as a foreshadowing of the character of the public career of the biographical subject. If this was the purpose of the genre in the Greco-Roman biographies, this is how a reader/hearer of Luke would most probably have taken the material of a similar nature in 1:5–4:15. The first section of the gospel, then, should be read as anticipation/prophecy/foreshadowing of the future career of Jesus. This material would foretell/foreshadow the type of person Jesus would be in his public ministry, which in Luke's narrative begins at 4:16.[55]

The expectations of Luke's audience for Jesus should be very high. It should not be surprising, then, to find this precocious boy, in his first recorded words, asking the sort of rhetorical question that we find in Luke 2:49: τί ὅτι ἐζητεῖτέ με; οὐκ ᾔδειτε ὅτι ἐν τοῖς τοῦ πατρός μου δεῖ εἶναί με; (How is it that you sought me? Did you not know that I must be in my Father's house?). The necessity in the question is not supported by an appeal to Scripture; however, already from 2:46–47, the Lukan audience knows that this young man has special insight and knowledge.

Using material found in Theon's progymnasmata, Paul Elbert has shown that Luke was very adept at using a question on the lips of a character as a hinge to connect the preceding material with what followed. He suggests that

> Luke fully realized that appropriately composed narrative-rhetorical questions can have a direct bearing on the comprehension of future words that are to be recorded after them. A number of Luke's dual-element questions (e.g., Acts 8:31) function directly to set the stage for further explanation,

---

55. Charles H. Talbert, *Reading Luke: A Literary and Theological Commentary on the Third Gospel* (Macon, Ga.: Smyth & Helwys, 2002), 17.

dialogue, instruction, action, prophecy, or speeches by his characters, just as a number of the short, one-clause questions do in both his books. Such questions allow a narrator to present further information through his characters that is of didactic value to his readers.[56]

Thus, the question Jesus poses to his parents both explains his present behavior and points forward to his future behavior: he stayed behind to be about his Father's business, the same activity that will occupy his later years. A story that involves a twelve year old boy speaking of the necessity of his presence in the Temple, which he calls "my Father's," requires preparation and development. Only the kind of introduction that Luke gives Jesus in Luke 1–2 can prepare the reader for this kind of question from the young lad.

In addition to the material in Luke 1–4 that prepares a reader for an exceptional claim, Luke 4–9 also helps in this respect. In that section of the Gospel, Jesus had performed many miracles, both fulfilling the expectations established in the opening section, and preparing the audience to accept his authority to make a claim such as the one found in 9:22. The audience has witnessed demons flee at Jesus' command (4:35); fish were caught when his command was obeyed (5:6); the paralytic regained his strength when Jesus' spoke (5:24–25); a withered hand was restored on the Sabbath by his word (6:10); a centurion's servant is healed when Jesus sends his word (7:7–10); his word calms the wind and waves (8:24); and at Jesus' command a legion of demons enter a herd of swine (8:32–33). The audience is also aware of the growing hostility toward Jesus (4:28–29; 5:30; 6:11). Taken together, these passages indicated the way in which Luke may have presented something incredible in a credible manner.

Also, it seems likely that Luke was telling his audience that Jesus' death was necessary in some positive sense. What better way to communicate this than in the mouth of a clearly extraordinary individual? The same material that serves to make the narrative credible can help a reader see that it is a positive outcome that Luke has in mind. It seems less likely that Luke was offering an apology for Jesus' ignoble death by claiming that he did not choose this; rather, it was forced upon him by necessity. Certainly, Luke's gospel thinks highly of Jesus and his sacrificial death, but Theon reminds us that we should not praise those who act out of necessity. Jesus'

---

56. Paul Elbert, "An Observation on Luke's Composition and Narrative Style of Questions," *CBQ* 66 (2003): 98–109 (104). A "dual-element question" is one in which the second part of the question refers back to the previous narrative and the first part of the question links forward with the following material. Elbert sees this type of question as a consistent feature in Luke. He sees Luke 2:46 as foregrounding the question in 2:49b.

statement about his impending death is both credible and serves to indicate that this necessity is a good thing. Could Luke be praising Jesus for doing something out of necessity? This would involve the overturning of a rhetorical convention.

In Acts, divine necessity plays a role in many important events, two of which will be singled out for examination here: the selecting of a replacement for Judas (Acts 1:12–26), and Paul's journey to Rome (Acts 19:21–28:31).

Divine Necessity: The Loss of Judas and His Replacement

In Acts 1, we can locate in the narrative the persons (Peter and the ten), action (selection of a replacement), place (upper room), time (after they had returned from Mt. Olivet), manner (willingly), cause (Judas' death). They have met in the upper room to select a replacement for Judas. Peter's speech (vv. 16–22) displays Luke's rhetorical skill. Twice in this account divine necessity influences the plot, 1:16 (ἔδει) and 1:21 (δεῖ). I mentioned this passage earlier to show the "necessary" connection between the ending of Luke and the beginning of Acts. Here, the net will be cast a bit wider. The questions we asked of Jesus' declaration of his death are relevant again here. Is Luke telling us this action was necessary for some good purpose? Is he offering us an excuse for the actions of the followers of Jesus? How is this account presented credibly?

The passage includes the first post-ascension speech by Peter, an act that establishes him as the spokesman for the group in the absence of Jesus, and inaugurates his authoritative role in the following narrative.[57] The problem is apparent to the reader of Luke-Acts: Judas who was one of the twelve was lost at the end of Luke's gospel. The list of apostles in Luke 6:16 and Acts 1:13 are the same, with the exception of the missing Judas, even though the order varies somewhat. Parsons has noticed this problem for Luke: "Before Luke narrates the fulfillment at Pentecost of Jesus' promise that the disciples will be empowered by the Holy Spirit, Luke addresses what was for him a problem of the first magnitude. The circle of the Twelve has been broken and must be restored."[58]

Luke's "must" becomes Peter's δεῖ because the plot requires an explanation of the loss of Judas. Jacques Dupont points out that Peter's explanation (1:21–22) of the second of the two prophecies he cites ("His office let another take," 1:20b) becomes

---

57. William H. Shepherd, Jr., *The Narrative Function of the Holy Spirit as a Character in Luke-Acts* (SBLDS 147; Atlanta, Ga.: Scholars Press, 1994), 158.

58. Mikeal Parsons, "Acts," in *Acts and Pauline Epistles* (ed. Watson E. Mills et al; Mercer Commentary on the Bible 7; Macon, Ga.: Mercer University Press, 1997), 1–64 (6).

programmatic for the apostolic community: *il faut qu'un autre soit substitute à l'apôtre apostat* (it is necessary that another be substituted for the apostate apostle).[59] The entire pericope (vv. 12–26) makes up a narrative that presents the problem and moves beyond it to include the solution. It is precisely in the "action" part of the narrative that we find δεῖ functioning most clearly.

This use of δεῖ is in good keeping with Theon's advice about the construction of a narrative. If we look closely at this narrative, other than perhaps advantage, no other property of action is relevant here. The "why" question, that may have lurked in the back of some readers' minds, is answered with a resounding "it must be!" The audience would understand that there were two prophetic passages in the Psalms: one that spoke of Judas' death and another of his replacement (1:20). As Peter states (1:16), these passages were places where "the Holy Spirit predicted through the mouth of David . . . ."

The Holy Spirit has declared beforehand (προεῖπεν) through the mouth of David concerning Judas. Therefore, just as certainly as the writing about Jesus must be fulfilled, so must the prophetic writings Peter cites (1:20) about Judas' loss of property (Ps 69:25) and his replacement within the Twelve (Ps 109:8). The logic is clear: the Holy Spirit declared through David that Judas' place would be lost, but the Holy Spirit also declared that someone else should take his place. An event that was predicted to happen (Judas' death and loss of property) points to an event that now has to happen (replacement).

Peter's claim of the prediction by the Holy Spirit gives us reason to ask about the Holy Spirit. This is the first time the Holy Spirit has become active in Acts. This is the Holy Spirit who was so active in the early chapters of Luke's gospel.[60] The Holy Spirit filled John the Baptist from his birth (1:15); overshadowed Mary (Luke 1:35); filled Elizabeth and Zechariah (1:41, 67); rested upon Simeon (2:25); revealed special information to Simeon (2:26); and descended upon Jesus and filled him (3:22 and 4:1). It is Shepherd's contention that "the Holy Spirit is best understood as a character in the narrative of Luke-Acts, and that the function of that character is to signal narrative reliability."[61] He also notes that the way in which the Holy Spirit is characterized in Luke-Acts, is also the way in which God is characterized. This,

---

59. Jacques Dupont, "La Destinée de Judas Prophétisée par David (Actes 1, 16–20)," *CBQ* 23/1 (1961): 41–51 (50).

60. Nine of the thirteen references to the Holy Spirit in Luke come in the first four chapters, with eight of those in the first three chapters.

61. Shepherd, *Narrative Function of the Spirit as a Character*, 247.

coupled with the activity of the Spirit mentioned above, points to the reliability of the statement made by Peter in Acts 1:16—what was spoken by the Spirit indeed *was* fulfilled (ἔδει πληρωθῆναι), and indeed *must be* fulfilled (δεῖ . . . γενέσθαι, 1:21–22).

Luke presents his readers with a credible account of the selection of a replacement for Judas. Instead of being a haphazard decision on the part of one or two disciples who may have wanted to seize the opportunity to pick *their* replacement for Judas, the event unfolds as one that had already been predicted by the Holy Spirit. The familiar activity of the Holy Spirit in the early chapters of Luke will remind the readers that the Spirit's predictions are correct. Luke is thereby presenting the action of choosing a replacement for Judas as a necessary action. This, for Luke, is a good thing. It is always a good thing according to Luke to go where the Spirit leads. It does not seem that Luke is presenting apostles as meeting under duress or due to necessity so that their actions are excused or somehow 'explained' to the audience. Since Peter is the spokesperson for this group, and since it is quite clear that Luke thinks highly of Peter, perhaps Theon's caution against praising those who act out of necessity is ignored by Luke. A similar tendency appears in relation to Paul in what follows.

Paul's Journey to Rome

The necessity of Paul's visit to Rome is presented in Acts 19:21; 23:11; and 27:24. In the first and last accounts, the words are Paul's; the words belong to Jesus in the middle account. Some scholars have been troubled by ἐν τῷ πνεύματι in 19:21, where Paul is described by "ἔθετο (aorist middle indicative of τίθημι) in the Spirit/spirit" regarding a decision about going to Jerusalem. Luke Timothy Johnson is unsure whether "Holy Spirit" is meant, so he translates the phrase ἔθετο ὁ Παῦλος ἐν τῷ πνεύματι as Paul "decided."[62] Joseph Fitzmyer flatly rejects the position that Holy Spirit is meant here. He translates, "put (it) in his spirit/mind," which uses the middle voice of τίθημι to indicate that it is a "question of Paul's' own *pneuma*."[63] On the other hand, Gerhard Schneider believes that Luke indicates by his phrase (ἔθετο . . . ἐν τῷ πνεύματι) that Paul *vornahm* in the Holy Spirit, that is, Paul resolved in the Holy Spirit or made a decision in definite collaboration with the Holy

---

62. Luke Timothy Johnson, *The Acts of the Apostles* (SP 5; Collegeville, Minn.: Liturgical, 1992), 346.

63. Joseph Fitzmeyer, *Acts of the Apostles* (AB 31; New York, N. Y.: Doubleday, 1998), 652.

Spirit. Schneider translates 19:21a accordingly as "Nach deisen Ereignissen nahm sich Paulus im Geiste vor," adding that "mit δεῖ verbundene Theologie des Planes Gottes; vlg. 23, 11; 27, 24."[64]

Why Paul determines to go to Rome is unclear,[65] especially in light of 18:2, which recounts that the Emperor Claudius had ordered all Jews to leave Rome, therefore it would seem incredible that Paul would want to go there. John Squires thinks that it has everything to do with the inevitable plan of God that unfolds in the Lukan narrative. The reader will remember that in Acts 9, divine necessity is thrust upon Paul by Jesus himself who declares that Paul will be told what he must do (ὅτι σε δεῖ ποιεῖν – 9:6) and how much he must suffer for the name of Jesus (ὅσα δεῖ αὐτὸν ὑπὲρ τοῦ ὀνόματός μου παθεῖν – 9:16). In light of this, Squires claims

> Just as Jesus must suffer, so must Paul; and just as Jesus had to go to Jerusalem to meet that fate, so Paul had to go to Rome . . . As in Hellenistic history, Fate is revealed in dreams, so on two occasions the Lord appears in epiphanies and affirms this necessity: 'you must (δεῖ) bear witness also at Rome' (23:11) and 'you must (δεῖ) stand before Caesar' (27:24)."[66]

However, remember that even though Luke uses "fate-like" language in δεῖ, his idea of necessity is related to the God of the OT. Parsons has noticed that Paul's language "is quite strong; Paul says he *must* see Rome, a word characteristically used in Acts to describe divine purpose."[67] Though this unit of narrative is only two verses, it prepares Luke's readers for the rest of Paul's ministry; it is the last eight chapters of Acts in overview.

This use of δεῖ by Luke may at first seem suspicious. After all, if Paul is determining to go "on his own," (*pneuma* = Paul's human spirit), then he is on shaky ground. The Lukan narrative, however, precludes this reading because Paul has already proven to be a character upon whom the Holy Spirit rests and through whom

---

64. Gerhard Schneider, *Die Apostelgeschichte II. Teil, Kommentar zu Kap. 9, 1 – 28, 31* (HTKNT 5/2; Freiburg: Herder, 1982), 271, 273.

65. Cosgrove, "Divine ΔΕΙ in Luke-Acts," 181, thinks it demonstrates that Paul, like Jesus before him, is not a passive pawn but "a creative executor of the divine δεῖ." From a narrative-critical perspective Günter Wasserberg, *Aus Israels Mitte – Heil für die Welt: Eine narrative-exegetische Studie zur Theologie des Lukas* (BZNW 92; Berlin: de Gruyter, 1998), 336, observes here something that Luke surely has in mind as well, namely that "Narrativ *zielt* das lukanische Erzählwerk gemäß Act 1, 8; 19, 21 auf Rom" (emphasis his).

66. John T. Squires, *The Plan of God in Luke-Acts* (Cambridge: Cambridge University Press, 1993), 174.

67. Parsons, "Acts," 48.

God works his will (Acts 9:22, 28; 13:2, 9; 14:1, 27; 15:12). Even though the reader is aware that Rome is a dangerous place for Paul, they can believe he must go because of the previous material by which Luke has set up this passage.

The firmness of the ground upon which Paul stands in making his prophetic, Spirit-inspired claim is further supported by two following events in which the claim is reaffirmed by divine beings. In the second account of Paul's visit to Rome where δεῖ is employed, Jesus speaks to Paul in a vision: Τῇ δὲ ἐπιούσῃ νυκτὶ ἐπιστὰς αὐτῷ ὁ κύριος εἶπεν· θάρσει ὡς γὰρ διεμαρτύρω τὰ περὶ ἐμοῦ εἰς Ἰερουσαλήμ, οὕτω σε δεῖ καὶ εἰς Ῥώμην μαρτυρῆσαι (The following night the Lord stood by him and said, "Take courage, for as you have testified about me at Jerusalem, so you must bear witness also at Rome" [23:11]). Here, we see that not only was Paul correct that he "must" see Rome, his insistence in 19:21 to go to Jerusalem proves to be in the divine plan as well. Johnson notes that the vision in which the divine δεῖ is found, "functions as a programmatic prophecy which shows the direction the plot will continue to take."[68] The words of Jesus, then, confirm the accuracy of Paul's earlier statement. Necessity in Luke-Acts appears to be quite significant to the story.

In the last account (27:24), Paul recounts a vision in which an angel of God stood by him and pronounced: μὴ φοβοῦ, Παῦλε, Καίσαρί, σε δεῖ παραστῆναι, καὶ ἰδοὺ κεχάρισταί σοι ὁ θεὸς πάντας τοὺς πλέοντας μετὰ σοῦ ("Do not be afraid, Paul; you must stand before Caesar; and lo, God has granted you all those who sail with you"). In this third statement concerning Paul's visit to Rome, an angel of the Lord "stands by" Paul, much as Jesus had "stood near" him in 23:11. In 27:24, Paul is told that he must "stand before" Caesar. Luke may be presenting his readers with a *paronomasia*.[69] In 27:23, Paul tells the men on board the ship that the angel παρέστη μοι (stood by me). The root is παρίστημι, which is also the word used in 27:24. However, in 9:41 and 24:13 παρίστημι means "to show to be true" or "to prove." Perhaps by means of this paronomasia, Luke is suggesting that not only will Paul go to Rome to "stand before" Caesar, but he will also "show to be true" the message that he will bring to the imperial city.[70] Thus, a second time Paul's initial statement, "After I have been there, I must (δεῖ) also see Rome"—preceded by Luke's

---

68. Johnson, *Acts*, 399.

69. Paranomasia is a figure of diction used when a word looks or sounds like another but has a different meaning.

70. This is certainly plausible given the ending of Acts: "And he lived there two whole years at his own expense, and welcomed all who came to him, preaching the kingdom of God and teaching about the Lord Jesus Christ quite openly and unhindered" (28:30–31). Nothing is mentioned of his visit to Caesar.

description of Spirit interaction, ἔθετο ὁ Παῦλος ἐν τῷ πνεύματι (19:21)—is shown to be true.

Luke overcomes the implausibility of Paul going to Rome in light of 18:2 by establishing Paul as a reliable character and by having divine beings reaffirm his statements. This is in keeping with Theon's directive to "state what is unbelievable in a believable way." The divine support given in Acts for the necessity of Paul's involvement with the Christian mission highlights that in the narrative, Luke is definitely presenting the action of Paul as necessary in a good sense. What makes it good is that this is what God wants for Paul; something that is reinforced in several ways. Again, it seems less than likely that Luke is offering an apology for Paul's ill-timed trip to Rome and for all the trouble he gets into there. The tone of the passage does not seem to be an excuse for Paul's behavior—he was forced to go—but one of praise for a man who was obedient to the voice of God. Luke clearly thinks highly of Paul, and by including necessity language in his narrative of Paul's actions, perhaps he is overturning the rhetorical convention of not praising those who act out of necessity. Perhaps for Luke and his audience who were familiar with the OT, obedience is the greatest virtue of all.

Conclusion

By taking into consideration Theon's *progymnasmata* when reading Luke-Acts, we can see how Luke's education informs his style. There is a rhetorical component to Luke's use of δεῖ. Although previous scholars have analyzed δεῖ and attempted to use a rhetorical-critical method in Luke-Acts, the specific element of necessity as an aspect of narrative events has not been examined.

Characters can speak with authority concerning necessity because they have been proven to be reliable. In some cases, as with Peter in Acts 1, a scriptural prophecy precedes and is the foundation of the argument from necessity. In other cases, as with Jesus in Luke 9, divine mandate (which may come through a dream, vision, or other epiphany) is coupled with other "signs" of the character's reliability. In the case of Paul's journey to Jerusalem, the apostle speaks first of the need to go, and only later are his words proven to be in accordance with God's plan via a visit from Jesus and the angel of the Lord.

Because we believe that Luke was very familiar with rhetoric, we can also believe that he knew of and used the rhetorical strategy of presenting certain actions as necessary. By so doing, he could move the narrative along by allowing Jesus, the

Holy Spirit, or certain characters to predict what must be done in the future, and thus how his story would unfold.

The other passages in Luke-Acts where δεῖ occurs, not to mention the others where divine necessity is present in the absence of δεῖ, need to be examined before a clear narrative-rhetorical use of divine necessity in Luke-Acts can be offered. For example, it is possible that Luke 11:42 is an example of necessity functioning as support for a thesis about tithing. It is worded in such a way that it is not directed at any particular group, though the Pharisees are immediately in view. Perhaps other passages in Luke-Acts will be discovered to reflect a similar rhetorical structure.

Acts of the Spirit:
Ezekiel 37 in the Light of Contemporary Speech-Act Theory

JACQUELINE GREY

jgrey@alphacrucis.edu.au
Alphacrucis College, Chester Hill, New South Wales, Australia

Introduction

> For to speak of God's new creation does indeed imply that God did once create the world but at the same time that this creation has also been so gravely impaired that a new creative act of God is needed to make good the seriousness of this damage.[1]

Ezekiel 37:1–14 anticipates the re-creation of the exilic community that has indeed been gravely impaired. The community is bereft of all hope. Yet into this valley of broken dreams steps the prophet to announce a coming restoration and transformation. The prophet is given a vision in which he declares, by the word of Yahweh, a re-creation of the broken community. He is directed by Yahweh to speak the very words that will achieve this change. As he speaks, the words of the prophet *do* something. In this vision, his words create a new reality. Prophetic speech is intended to transform, rather than simply inform.[2] Speech-act theory has long recognized that words achieve more than simply the transmission of information. Communication is an action that achieves certain results.

This study is an examination of the contribution of speech-act theory to biblical studies. In particular, it examines this theory as applied to the narrative of Ezekiel 37:1–14. While it may be a creative leap to apply a pragmatic theory to a religious text,[3] the benefits are enormous—particularly for the insights into the activity of the

---

1. Hans Hübner, "The Holy Spirit in Holy Scripture," *Ecumenical Review* 41/3 (1989): 324–38 (333).

2. Matthias Wenk, "The Creative Power of the Prophetic Dialogue," *Pneuma* 26/1 (2004): 118–29 (119).

3. Daniel Patte, "Speech-Act Theory and Biblical Exegesis," *Semeia* 41 (1988): 85–102 (100).

spirit that this method highlights. Through this study, the role of the *ruach*, or Spirit, emerges as a mysterious force that works to achieve the re-creation of the despairing community through the words of the prophet, inspiring hope and life.

Speech-act Theory

Speech-act theory was first developed by John L. Austin in his 1962 essay "How to do things with Words." While his work has since been developed for religious language and texts by later scholars (including Thistleton, Vanhoozer and Briggs), at the heart of Austin's theory is the idea that speech is performative. As Houston notes, a major contribution of speech-act theory is the recognition that language is not just referential and informative.[4] Words are often employed for more than just description or simple declaration of fact. When a marriage celebrant says "I now pronounce you husband and wife," it is more than a statement of fact. The words of this authorized celebrant change the status of the two single people in the eyes of the community so that they are now one in marriage. Language and speech *does* something. The statement of the celebrant *makes* what is said a fact and a new reality.[5] So it is possible to ask of any utterance, "What is *being done* when that is said?"[6] While the performance of words might be easy to identify in ritualistic speech (such as a wedding ceremony), how does it work in other contexts? Austin identified three core elements within any speech act. In general, any speech act or utterance will contain a locutionary, illocutionary and perlocutionary dimension.

Firstly, each statement of utterance must make sense. That is, the statement must have meaning. This is the locutionary dimension. Any utterance needs to be understood—it must a legitimate use of words in a language that makes recognizable sense. It must conform to basic grammar and communication rules—it cannot be gibberish.[7] It is *what* we are saying.

But a meaningful statement is usually more than just a transaction of information. A speech act, secondly, is generally more than merely saying something to fill up space; we *do* something in the act. We ask questions, we promise, we threaten,

---

4. Walter Houston, "What did the Prophets think they were doing? Speech acts and prophetic discourse in the Old Testament," *BibInt* 1/2 (1993): 167–88 (170).

5. Dan R. Stiver, *The Philosophy of Religious Language: Sign, Symbol & Story* (Oxford: Blackwell, 1996), 80.

6. Houston, "What did the Prophets think?," 171.

7. Stiver, *Philosophy*, 81.

we make appointments, we instruct, we plead, we persuade, we give assurances, we excuse. This is called the illocutionary dimension of the speech act. As Stiver notes, it is identified with what we do *in* saying something.[8] The illocutionary force of a speech act can also be identified with the intention of the speaker or writer. This does not mean that they achieve their intended outcome, but it recognizes the intended aim of their communication. For example, a "friend" was recently preaching at a local church in a neighbouring city. As this friend was unknown to the congregation she decided to begin the message with a funny story. In presenting this story, her intention (or illocution) was to establish some warmth and rapport with the audience. However as she gave the punch-line, the humor of the story was lost on the audience. The (perlocutionary) effect was not the intended rapport but a slight hostility that she then had to work hard to overcome! In this sense, the perlocutionary effect was unsuccessful (or what Austin would call "unhappy"). The speech act had misfired. In any speech act, generally there is a sense of intention; even if it does not achieve its aim. This dimension is complicated by the fact that in the case of many other communications we cannot know for sure what the speaker (or author) actually intended—especially when it comes to written texts. Yet, we can sometimes get insight into the intention of a speech act by the effect that it creates. This is particularly true if it has a perlocutionary effect (what is done *by* the saying) in which both the speaker and audience remain "happy" with the outcome.

Yet understanding the illocutionary force of a speech act is not necessarily tied to the intention of the speaker in the same way as authorial-intention hermeneutics[9] understands it. It is not about reconstructing the mind of the original author, but interpreting the authorial discourse.[10] As Wolterstorff asserts, "Authorial-discourse interpretation is interpretation aimed at discerning what the speaker or writer said—that is to say, which illocutionary act he or she performed." It aims to understand what the author or speaker did in their communication.[11] The intention of the speaker is not something that is marked in the text itself. Instead it is a gap (or an absence) that the reader has to fill in order to make sense of the text.[12] The intention

---

8. Ibid.

9. Nicholas Wolterstorff, "The Promise of Speech-act Theory for Biblical Interpretation" in *After Pentecost: Language and Biblical Interpretation* (ed. Craig G. Bartholomew, Colin J. D. Greene, and Karl Möller; Grand Rapids, Mich.: Zondervan, 2001), 73–90 (75).

10. Wolterstorff, "Promise," 82.

11. Ibid.

12. Patte, "Speech-Act Theory," 91.

can, in some instances, be read through the overall communicative act to observe all elements of the speech act; what was said, the effect of the speech act, and the response of the speaker to the effect.

For example, the overall communication in Ezekiel 37:1–14 is a narrative in which speech acts are embedded. To understand the illocutionary force of the speech acts, we can observe the effect this has (the perlocutionary effect), and then observe the response of the speaker within the narrative to this outcome. Combined with narrative criticism, we can see in the story the effect of the words of the prophet. Does the narrative present the prophet as being happy with the effect? Were they surprised or distressed by the outcome? If not, it is quite possible that their speech act has been successful. In asking what the causal effect of the speech act achieves, we are asking about the perlocutionary effect of the communication. The perlocutionary effect is the third element in Austin's speech-act theory.

The perlocutionary effect is something that is done *by* the saying. Although a speaker may intend (illocutionary dimension) to persuade, he cannot force the audience to be persuaded. The effect is unpredictable. If the effect on the audience is as intended, then the perlocutionary effect is successful. The perlocutionary effect of the speech act of the wedding celebrant is to change the situation of two single people to a legal couple in the public domain. An alternative example given by Stiver is someone who intends to persuade another person to flee by means of a warning. If that person does indeed flee, then the effect and intention correlate—the communicative act has been successful. One of the benefits of Austin's theory is that it differentiates between what is done *in* saying, and what is done *by* saying.[13] It affirms that language can transform as well as inform.[14] However it must be asked what other factors contribute to a successful speech act. If any unregistered person at the wedding ceremony stood up and declared the two single people "husband and wife" would it be a legitimate speech act? Could these same words be uttered by an unauthorized person and have the same effect? Would it have the same perlocutionary effect?

A crucial element in this discussion is the role of the "speaker." If the effect of some speech is to change the reality of the world, it cannot be just anyone who utters the speech act. The speaker must have the authority to make that change; usually through their social or institutional role. This is the interlocutionary role or social

---

13. Stiver, *Philosophy*, 81.

14. Kevin J. Vanhoozer, "From Speech Acts to Scripture Acts: The Covenant of Discourse and the Discourse of Covenant," in *After Pentecost*, 1–49 (6).

dimension of speech acts.[15] As Vanhoozer writes, ". . . communicative actions involve much more than a linguistic code or the shear meaning of words. They involve communicative agents taking responsibility for what they do with their words."[16] The role of authority and responsibility becomes increasingly important when we turn to the prophetic text of Ezekiel 37:1–14. What gives the prophets legitimacy in their speech act is their authority as the spokesperson of Yahweh. They speak the words given to them by Yahweh. Each meaningful statement of utterance by the prophets comes not of their own volition, but at the direction of Yahweh. As noted by Houston, there are several indications in the prophetic texts that demonstrate the belief that words are capable of accomplishing the task of which it speaks. Texts such as Jeremiah 5:14; Hosea 6:5; Isaiah 55:11 point to the power of words for achieving something. However these words achieve outcomes precisely because they are the words of Yahweh, mediated through the spokesperson. The prophets speak on behalf of God and therefore have the authority of God.[17] It is within this dynamic that we can also explore what Wolfterstorff describes as the "double-agency discourse." He writes,

> Paradigmatic cases are those in which one person has been deputized to speak on behalf of another, so that the latter performs an illocutionary act by way of the former performing some locutionary act (and perhaps some illocutionary act as well), as well as those cases in which one person performs some illocutionary act by way of appropriating the illocutionary act of another.[18]

While Wolterstorff uses this approach to describe "Divine discourse"—how God speaks to us through Scripture—it has implications for prophetic texts. Wolterstorff's method could suggest that deputized speakers, such as prophets, are automaton machines without personality or input into the speech they deliver on Yahweh's behalf. Instead, through this study we will see that the illocutionary act gives us insight into the role of the prophets and their role as spokespersons. The illocutionary force of the prophets differentiates them from Yahweh as their words have a different purpose and role—otherwise they would be unnecessary.

---

15. Ibid., 17.
16. Ibid.
17. Houston, "What did the Prophets think?," 169.
18. Wolterstorff, "Promise," 83.

Yet is speech-act theory reduced only to speech? Thistleton asks whether speech-act theory can be applied to written texts. The response is further complicated by the consideration of the oral origins of most of the biblical text—they are written texts of speech acts. This refers not only to situations of oral or recorded speech, but even some written documents (such as written promises, legal wills, etc) that can *do* something (or have an effect) in the public domain, and hence function as effective *acts*.[19] These types of writing are evident in the biblical text, which contains not only recorded speech but also written promises, acts of cursing and judgment and acts of blessing, acts of repentance and acts of worship.[20] The text of Ezekiel 37:1–14 is a narrative report of a visionary experience of the prophet. Does it present a speech act? Embedded within this narrative are several events of recorded speech, which do indeed present a speech act, albeit a recorded and now static event. However to understand the specific occurrences of speech acts in this text, let us consider the broader narrative of 37:1–14.

The Narrative Report of Ezekiel 37:1–14

The book of Ezekiel reports the ministry of the prophet to the community.[21] In particular, in 37:1–14, it reports the vision given to reinforce to the prophet his own role in the restoration of the nation. His words will "effect" their future and help to bring about their re-creation as promised by Yahweh. The report of the vision of the valley of dry bones is presented as a first person narrative. It begins with the "hand of Yahweh" taking the prophet to this unspecific place[22] of defeat and death. The prophet-priest is placed in a valley of unclean bones, yet does not appear troubled by exposing himself and associating with these unclean elements. He and Yahweh walk—not in the garden, like the original creation in Genesis 2—but through a garden of death. It is a picture of absolute despair. Yahweh asks: "can these bones live?" (v. 3). The restrained response of the prophet ("You know") reveals a sense of powerlessness.[23] The picture also gives an indication of the self-esteem (or lack thereof)

---

19. Anthony C. Thistleton, *New Horizons in Hermeneutics: The Theory and Practice of Transforming Biblical Reading* (Grand Rapids, Mich.: Zondervan, 1992), 17.

20. Ibid., 17–18.

21. Ronald M. Hals, *Ezekiel* (FOTL 19; Grand Rapids, Mich.: Eerdmans, 1989), 4.

22. For a historical overview of the discussion on the possible location of this valley, see Walther Zimmerli, *Ezekiel 2* (Hermeneia; trans. James D. Martin; ed. Paul D. Hanson with Leonard J. Greenspoon; Philadelphia, Pa.: Fortress, 1983), 258–59.

23. Ibid., 260.

of the people of ancient Israel. They saw themselves as being these very bones—dry, without life and without hope. Indeed, according to verse 11, this is what they are quoted with having said of their situation. The people's view of themselves clearly places this (shaped) material in the exilic period of the broader narrative of Ezekiel. As Zimmerli writes "The prophet's word in 37:1–14 is directed towards the community which sighs in deepest need in exile after 587 and which feels that it is at the end of all its hope."[24]

The final unit of vv. 11–14 makes it clear that the bones viewed by the prophet are symbolic of Israel. This scene of death was in reality a metaphor. Exile is not just a removal from their homeland or a military defeat; exile is their death.[25] It is also clear that they cannot by their own self-improvement alter the situation of death and despair. The bones appear beyond hope of life. It will take a miracle to restore them. There is no hope of restoration as a normal process (v. 3). It will take a radical intervention and re-creation of Yahweh.[26] But that is exactly what Yahweh offers them. The narrative presents a restoration miracle in which the bones come together and are given form and life. This is what Yahweh offers them through the prophet—a re-creation. Through the following disputation of vv. 11–14, Yahweh counters the resigned despair of the people with a message of hope.[27] The promise of re-creation that he offers is true salvation as it reverses the previous evil situation.[28] It will reverse the pronouncement (what Zimmerli calls the curse) of Hosea 1:9 that they are "not my people" and restore them to relationship with Yahweh.[29]

The restoration miracle[30] (vv. 4–10) is divided into two clear phases. In the first phase the scattered bones come together and are reconstructed to the form of the body (vv. 4–8). In the second phase they are given breath and life (vv. 9–10). As Hals notes, this new (or re-) creation of the people of God deliberately mirrors the original creation in Genesis 2 that had earlier also depicted a two phase event. In the original creation, the form of the human was created, and then these forms were

---

24. Ibid., 265.

25. Christopher R. Seitz, "Ezekiel 37:1–14," *Int* 46/1 (1992): 53–56 (54–55).

26. Wonsuk Ma, "The Spirit of God in Creation: Lessons for Christian Mission," *Transformation* 24/3–4 (2007): 222–30 (225).

27. Zimmerli, *Ezekiel*, 257.

28. Hals, *Ezekiel*, 269–70.

29. Zimmerli, *Ezekiel*, 266.

30. Hals, *Ezekiel*, 269.

given life by the breath of the Spirit of Yahweh. The giving of the Spirit took place after the forming of the body.[31] Without God's Spirit there could be no life.[32]

These two phases of the restoration miracle in Ezekiel 37 present four speech acts. Each act of the forming of the bodies and then the infusion of life into the bodies is preceded by two speech acts. The first is the speech of Yahweh (vv. 4–6), the second speech act is the speech of the prophet (v. 7). Yahweh instructs the prophet with the words to deliver as his authoritative spokesperson. It is only after both speech acts (of Yahweh *and* the prophet) that the perlocutionary effect of their speech is evident. Through proclamation a change is effected. As Zimmerli writes of the role of the prophet:

> He is to address the dead bones in an instructive proclamatory oracle. . . . Then, now, precisely in the imperative, he is to proclaim once again the divine command to "the spirit of life" with all his prophetic power (v. 9). Under the influence of this activity on the part of the preacher there begins to emerge, within the visionary experience, life from death.[33]

Zimmerli highlights that it is the words of the prophet that produce the perlocutionary effect of change in the situation of the dry bones to bring them to life, not the words of Yahweh. In the original creation it is Yahweh who forms the human then breathes the *ruach* of life into the body. But now, in this re-creation, it is not Yahweh who performs this role, but the prophet. Yahweh directs the prophet to speak, but it is only as the prophet actually speaks that a change in the bones occurs. The prophet participates in the divine activity in a crucial role.[34] He is not a bystander or a peripheral figure, but he authoritatively commands (an illocutionary act) the divine agency of the *ruach* to complete "his" words (the locutionary act). The *ruach* responds to the illocutionary force of the prophet (speaking the words of Yahweh), not to Yahweh directly.

The exact derivation of the term *ruach* in this text has been a subject of much debate. In Ezekiel 37, *ruach* occurs ten times in fourteen verses. This locutionary dynamic has been widely discussed. The term could equally be understood to mean either "wind," "breath," or "spirit." Yet, such a clean separation into options is rejected by Seitz. He writes, "Yahweh's spirit is at once Israel's breath and at the same time a

---

31. Ibid.
32. Seitz, "Ezekiel 37:1–14," 53.
33. Zimmerli, *Ezekiel*, 257.
34. Ibid.

wind gathered from the four compass points."[35] The image of wind suggests something of the mysterious, unpredictable, invisible, dynamic power of God.[36] Wind and breath are invisible and are only known by their effects (cf. John 3:8).[37] The text seems to deliberately blur the definitions of the term. This "spirit of life" seems to be regarded as something which permeates and comes from the whole of creation as the prophet calls the four winds to do the work that in the original creation was the work of the Spirit of God.[38] Now in this re-creation, as Seitz notes, the four winds are the Spirit of God. In this sense, the reference to the spirit refers to the presence and activity of God. The very ambiguity of terminology safeguards God's mystery.[39] This wind-spirit-breath comes as a response to the illocutionary force of the prophet. The wind-spirit-breath achieves the perlocutionary effect of the prophet's speech. But as the prophet utters these words, the effect is unpredictable to the prophet. The wind-spirit-breath is only seen by the perlocutionary effect. That effect is outside the control of the prophet. So how are the three dynamics of speech-act theory (locutionary, illocutionary and perlocutionary) specifically identified in the text? What is the actual effect of the prophet's speech?

Speech Acts in Ezekiel 37:1–14

As noted above, the locutionary dynamic is the basic meaning of the words and sentence construction. While this may not seem to have much initial significance in speech-act theory, what is important to note in Ezekiel 1:1–14 is that the speech of both Yahweh and the prophet in the two-phase miracle is presented as almost identical. This is an example of Wolterstorff's "double-agency discourse." Yahweh speaks the instructions to the prophet, as the spokesperson of Yahweh. From the narrative, the prophet is understood to have spoken these same words given by Yahweh, verbatim. However this is not what the text actually says. Whether this is for the purposes of brevity or part of a narrative technique, we are simply told that Ezekiel prophesied as he was commanded. We are told as part of the narrative that he spoke the same words of Yahweh. While the text suggests that their speech was

---

35. Seitz, "Ezekiel 37:1–14," 53.

36. John Goldingay, "Was the Holy Spirit Active in Old Testament Times? What was New About the Christian Experience of God?," *Ex Auditu* 12 (1996): 14–28 (15).

37. Ibid., 18.

38. Zimmerli, *Ezekiel*, 261.

39. Goldingay, "Was the Holy Spirit Active?," 18.

identical, their actual recorded locutionary acts are different. This difference in their locutionary act highlights the role of the prophet. He is not a machine that simply outputs command functions. Although he responds in obedience to the instruction of Yahweh, the prophet is still a separate person with a separate voice and volition. He may speak the same words, but what is recorded (his locutionary act), his intention (his illocutionary act), and the effect of his words (his perlocutionary effect), are quite different to Yahweh. He does not appropriate the illocutionary force of Yahweh, but instead presents a new illocutionary act with a new intention. This is particularly highlighted by the illocutionary force of his words.

Yahweh instructs the prophet saying: "Prophesy to these bones and say to them. . ." (v. 4). But the words he is given to speak are not just any words—he was to speak Yahweh's word. Ezekiel is instructed to speak a specific word to the bones. He was to speak a message of life over these bones that they would come together and join, that muscles and flesh would grow on them, and they would be restored to life. The illocutionary force of Yahweh's word is an instruction. When Yahweh speaks the words for the bones to come together nothing happens to the bones. When Yahweh speaks, the bones remain still, because although his words address them, his speech act is instructing the prophet. So when Yahweh gives this instruction, something happens to the prophet. He is enlivened with anticipation of his task. It requires daring, risk, and obedience to partner with God. It requires courage to hear God's voice and speak it. The illocutionary force of Yahweh's speech is to instruct the prophet; the perlocutionary effect of the speech act is the obedience of the prophet. Despite his sense of powerlessness, the prophet chooses to respond in obedience: he performs the command. He speaks the words of Yahweh as he was commanded (v. 7). So when Yahweh spoke, the bones remained dry and still. Now that the prophet speaks (at the instruction of Yahweh) announcing the word of Yahweh, the bones become animated. The words spoken by Yahweh and the prophet, we understand from the text, are identical. But the illocutionary force of the prophet is different. What is the illocutionary difference?

There is a difference in the illocutionary act of Yahweh and the illocutionary act of prophet—though it suggests the same words were used. Yahweh is instructing the speaker and not "prophesying." He does not perform the same illocutionary act as the prophet. In contrast, the prophet's speech is a declarative to the bones. A declarative brings about a change in one's world through one's utterance. It alters the state of affairs in reality.[40] When the prophet spoke this word, there was an extraor-

---

40. Houston, "What did the Prophets think?," 173.

dinary effect. As Zimmerli notes, ". . . the prophet is suddenly transformed from being the spokesman of human impotence into the spokesman of divine omnipotence."[41] Unlike the original creation (Gen 1) in which *ruach* Elohim simply spoke it into being, Yahweh now chooses to partner with and work through humanity, the stewards of his creation. The human agent is instrumental in fulfilling the purposes of Yahweh. The words of the prophet result in the energizing of the bones to form and be enlivened by the *ruach*. But is his speech act successful? As we observe the response of the prophet to the restoration of the bones, does the narrative present him as happy with the effect? Was he surprised or hurt by the outcome? He expresses no grief with the outcome. He accepts the transformation of the bones into a living army through his words without vocalizing any distress. The illocutionary force of his declarative has been successful. However if he evidences any surprise, it is not that the wind-spirit-breath has re-created the bones into a life force, but his surprise concerns what this life force represents: "a vast army" (v. 10).

The perlocutionary result of Yahweh's words is for the prophet to speak. Yahweh commands the prophet to speak, and he does. Yahweh's illocutionary force has been successful. However the perlocutionary result of the prophet's speech is in the activity of the *ruach* to re-create the bones into the vast army. The speech of the prophet *changes* something. This is more than just description; the speech act brings change to the world that matches the uttered words. The speech act of the prophet makes what is said a fact or reality. His breath (*ruach*) produces the reality, which is actuated by the Spirit (*ruach*). The Spirit (*ruach*) inhabits the breath (*ruach*) of the prophet's declaration, and works to achieve and fulfill the declaration. It is the prophet's declaration that has brought about the process of bodily "assembly." It is then at the second declaration of the prophet that causes the coming of the *ruach* into the lifeless bodies.[42] The words of the prophet have creative and "exercitive" force. The perlocutionary effect within the vision is a re-creation and restoration of the bones. What the *ruach* performs in this vision is promised for the world of the exilic community (vv. 11–14).

This work of the Spirit takes on an eschatological dimension as it looks forward to the fulfillment of the promise in which the nation will be restored and "resurrected." As Ma notes, "Before the coming of the Spirit in Ezek 37, the community had no life, but through the power of the Spirit, they become alive and ready to serve as

---

41. Zimmerli, *Ezekiel*, 26.
42. Ma, "Spirit of God in Creation," 225.

a living community of God."[43] In this sense, the vision of the bones (dead Israel) addresses the current Israel about their role, responsibility and future.[44] The narrative invites the trust and confidence of the community in Yahweh's ability to restore the exilic community. The result of the speech act of the prophet, within this vision, is transformation. This vision then becomes the basis of a promise from Yahweh to the actual world of the exilic community of Yahweh's intentions for them. He promises them a restoration equal to the re-creation of the bones in Ezekiel's vision.

Acts of the Spirit

While it is the speech act of the prophet that results in the restoration of the life of the bones, the passage is equally clear that the agent of the perlocutionary effect is the *ruach*. This re-creative power of the *ruach* brings about the transformation. The words of the prophet are the signal for the present but dormant *ruach* to be activated. Once the declarative is uttered by the prophet, the *ruach* begins to work. The perlocutionary effect is achieved only by the *ruach*. It is the breath of the prophet, which is the word of Yahweh, which is the wind from creation, which is the spirit that produces the perlocutionary effect. This effect is restorative; the *ruach* replaces death and despair with new life and hope. As Ma observes, ". . . it brings about fertility and prosperity, physical wholeness, and also moral transformation in society."[45] The ruach is at work within creation to make creation, in this instance Israel, alive again.[46] This wind-spirit-breath works not only to create (Genesis 1) but also to re-create. The action of the *ruach* has produced an unpredictable outcome. The creative result of the activity and presence of the *ruach* surprises the prophet. The prophet is not surprised that the word of Yahweh has been successful, but is surprised by what the Spirit creates. The image of the army (or host) is not a representation of renewed warfare and rearmament. It is a picture of a large number that will physically arise from the dust onto their feet with dignity, vitality and renewed pride.[47] Yet the *ruach* is a mystery; she does all this without been seen.[48]

---

43. Ibid., 228.
44. Thistleton, *New Horizons*, 274–75.
45. Ma, "Spirit of God in Creation," 227.
46. Hübner, "Holy Spirit in Holy Scripture," 331.
47. Zimmerli, *Ezekiel*, 262.
48. Given that *ruach is* a feminine noun in biblical Hebrew, a feminine personification seems appropriate.

The *ruach* does not speak, but the evidence of her presence is plain. The wind-spirit-breath is not seen, but makes things move.[49] The *ruach* remains hidden and mysterious—she is only known by her effects. Yet, the spirit responds to those in obedient relationship with Yahweh. The *ruach* acts in response to the speech and intentions of others (illocutionary act), including in the narrative Yahweh and Yahweh's prophet. In responding to the words of Yahweh spoken by the prophet, she points to Yahweh. She is active to ensure the fulfillment of the word of Yahweh rather than her own prestige. Her work is to glorify others. Del Colle asserts that "The Spirit's presencing is donative and life giving but self-effacing in regard to the Spirit's own Person."[50] Yet, like the prophet, she is not an automaton machine. She does not just output the data commands like a computer. The *ruach* achieves the results of the declaration of the prophet, but in a way that is creative, fresh and unpredictable. She re-creates and enlivens the bones in response to the word of Yahweh, but how she does it and what she forms is unexpected. She creates even beyond the expectations of the prophet. Yet she creates within the boundaries of the scope given in the declaration to produce a surprising effect; an army. It is almost as though the *ruach* takes creative liberties with the word of Yahweh. The *ruach* cannot be domesticated. The effect is to remind the prophet (and the people) of the power and vitality of the word of Yahweh. Yet the ruach also provides comfort. The final effect of this picture—a large host of re-dignified people created by the ruach—inspires hope within the prophet. However, while we can see the evidence of the *ruach* who works to achieve the perlocutionary effect of the speech act of the prophet, this does not tell us who the *ruach* is. Her actions tell us not who the *ruach* is, but more what the *ruach* does. But, like a detective, from this study of what the *ruach* does, we can create a picture of what and who the *ruach* is.

Conclusion

As Hübner notes, the nature and function of the *ruach* in biblical thinking are not terminologically separated. The essence and being of the *ruach* becomes clear through observation of what the *ruach* does.[51] From the above study, the *ruach* not only acts, but *is* creative, transformational and mysterious. The creativity of the *ruach* works to

---

49. Ralph Del Colle, "The Holy Spirit: Presence, Power, Person," *TS* 62 (2001): 322–40 (326).
50. Ibid., 333.
51. Hübner, "Holy Spirit in Holy Scripture," 325.

not only construct but inspire life. The form and effect of the wind-spirit-breath are identical; life and hope. Yet the creativity of the *ruach* is not mundane or predictable, but fresh and unexpected. The wind-spirit-breath comes from the four corners of the creation it has wrought to re-create life. The *ruach*, within the boundaries of the word of Yahweh, does not abandon the material of the bones but recycles what had no life to form a new existence. The raw material of the bones is transformed into a new people. This transformational nature of the *ruach* results in restoration. It is not enough to simply re-create Ezekiel's people from dry bones into living bones; they are transformed as a result. Having been through the shame of exile, they are now being transformed from "not my people" into the people of Yahweh once again. They are transformed from being defeated and unclean into a people with dignity and hope. The wind-spirit-breath comes from the four corners of creation to transform them. This is what the *ruach* does because this is who the wind-spirit-breath is; a transformational force. The ruach does all this without being seen; she is mysterious and self-effacing. She prefers the prestige and the accolades of her actions to go to another. She acts to empower others. The *ruach* is not self-promoting. In this humility, the *ruach* identifies with what she has created; the people in this vast army that she has formed are nameless, yet dignified. To create this army, she acts out of loving concern for the speech and intentions of others. But she does not respond to just any speech or intention; the *ruach* will work to bring to realization and promote the word of Yahweh. This is the 'acts of the spirit' in Ezekiel 37:1–14; the *ruach* acts (or functions) out of her character and nature—who she is.

Spirit-Gifted Callings in the Pauline Corpus, Part I: The Laying On of Hands

JOHN C. POIRIER

poirier@siscom.net
Kingswell Theological Seminary, Middletown, Ohio 45044

The laying on of hands appears two or three times in the Pastoral Epistles. In 1 Tim 4:14, the author[1] admonishes Timothy not to neglect the gift within him "which was given ... through prophecy with the laying on of hands of the elders." A somewhat different hand-laying rite is mentioned in 2 Tim 1:6: "I remind you to rekindle the gift of God that is within you through the laying on of my hands." I say "two or three times" because there is also a reference to the laying on of hands in 1 Tim 5:22, although it has recently been argued that this verse refers to an accusatory gesture, in which case it should not be brought alongside 1 Tim 4:14 and 2 Tim 1:6.[2] In what follows, I am mainly concerned with the difference between 1 Tim 4:14 and 2 Tim 1:6. I will also attempt to describe, in pneumatological terms, what took place during the latter.

A comparison between 1 Tim 4:14 and 2 Tim 1:6 prompts a series of questions. Do these verses refer to two different occasions? If so, why would Timothy need to have had hands laid on him twice? On the other hand, if they refer to the same occasion, then why is it described once as the laying on of the *elders'* hands, but a second

---

1. Even stylistic studies disagree on the question of the authorship of the Pastoral epistles, with David L. Mealand opposing Pauline authorship ("The Extent of the Pauline Corpus: A Multivariate Approach," *JSNT* 59 [1995]: 61–92), and linguistic analysis by Matthew Brook O'Donnell (*Corpus Linguistics and the Greek of the New Testament* [New Testament Monographs 6; Sheffield: Sheffield Phoenix, 2005], 88–90, 91–92, 96–99, 387–93) and by Armin D. Baum ("Semantic Variation within the *Corpus Paulinum*: Linguistic Considerations Concerning the Richer Vocabulary of the Pastoral Epistles," *TynB* 59/2 [2008]: 271–92) consistent with Pauline authorship. Fortunately, the question of authorship is largely immaterial for our study.

2. Brian P. Irwin argues that "lay hands on" in 1 Tim 5:22 refers to an accusatory gesture, similar to the use of this phrase to mean "arrest" or "strike against" in the OT and elsewhere in the NT ("The Laying on of Hands in 1 Timothy 5:22: A New Proposal," *BBR* 18 [2008]: 123–29). Even if Irwin is wrong, there is little call for the NRSV rendering of this verse as "Do not ordain anyone hastily, ..."
—interpretation should *follow* translation, not *precede* it.

time as the laying on of *Paul's* hands? In what follows, I will argue that 1 Tim 4:14 and 2 Tim 1:6 refer not only to two different occasions, but also to two altogether different rites. The laying on of the elders' hands is a rite of identification—it constitutes the means by which the community identifies Timothy as representative of them, and of their gospel. Some might call this "ordination," but that term is ultimately not very helpful for understanding what makes this rite so different from that of 2 Timothy. The latter does not involve the communal context of Timothy's ministry, but rather represents the means by which a real spiritual unction is passed from Paul to Timothy. In the rite from 1 Timothy, Timothy's gain comes by purely symbolic means, while the rite from 2 Timothy has to do with a real, spiritual impartation—a genuine flow of charismatic unction from one person to another.

It would help my argument that 1 Tim 4:14 and 2 Tim 1:6 refer to two different hand-laying rites if such rites were already differentiated elsewhere. It is widely recognized, in fact, that this is the case. In the OT, there are rites in which the point of the hand-laying was to establish an identification (in the sense of ritual representation) between those who are laying their hands and the one on whom the hands are laid, but there are also rites involving a transfer of something (in a more-than-symbolic sense) from one party to another.

Laying On of Hands in the Old Testament

In the OT, the laying on of hands appears almost exclusively in priestly writings. It is found most often in connection with peace, sin and burnt offerings (Exod 29:10, 15, 19; Lev 1:4; 3:2, 8, 13; 4:4, 15, 24, 29, 33; 8:14, 18, 22; Num 8:12; 2 Chron 29:23). It also appears in the case of the scapegoat ceremony (Lev 16:21), in the setting aside of the Levites for service (Num 8:10), in Moses' appointment of Joshua as his successor (Num 27:18, 23; Deut 34:9), and, in a very different sense, in connection with arresting, striking, or accusing (Exod 24:11; Lev 24:14; 2 Kgs 11:16; 2 Chron 23:15).[3]

For more than fifty years now, the discussion of the laying on of hands has turned on the distinction, argued by David Daube, between two Hebrew verbs used to refer to the act of "laying" the hands.[4] Daube claimed there is a big difference between "a real 'leaning on'" (סמך, *samakh*) of the hands and "a gentle 'placing'"

---

3. This last category appears in the NT as well: Matt 21:46 // Luke 20:19; Matt 26:50 // Mark 14:46; Luke 21:12; John 7:30, 44; 8:20; Acts 4:3; 5:18; 21:27; and (possibly) 1 Tim 5:22 (see n. 2). It is really only on a linguistic level that this is a laying on of hands—the expression is a euphemism.

4. David Daube, *The New Testament and Rabbinic Judaism* (Jordan Lectures in Comparative Reliigon 2; London: Athlone, 1956).

(שִׂים, *shim* or שִׁית, *shith*) of the hands on the object of the rite's attention. He associates the former with rites involving a transfer from one party to another, and the latter with rites of identification.[5] Thus, according to Daube's typology, there are essentially two categories of hand-laying rites: (1) the *leaning* of hands exemplified in Moses' ordination of Joshua, which belongs to the same essential type as the communal sacrifice (in which the high priest *leans* his hands upon the sacrificial victim), and (2) the *placing* of hands on the one receiving a commission, or something similar. The former could be found then, "at least up to the first half of the 2nd cent. A.D.," in the rite of ordination, in which the effect of the laying on of hands did not represent merely a symbolic identification between parties, but rather something more real. Daube points to the description for this rite found in *Numbers Rabba* (a text considerably later than the 2nd cent. CE): Moses is there described as being "like one pouring from vessel to vessel."[6] Moses' ordination of Joshua and the high priests' transfer of sins to the scapegoat do essentially the same thing: they "creat[e] ... a substitute."[7] But it is important to note Daube's use of the word "create." He has in mind something much more than a simple act of designation.

As the verb *samakh* is used in connection with the sacrificial offering, the scapegoat ceremony, and Moses' passing his mantle to Joshua, Daube assumes that

---

5. On this distinction, see Jacob Milgrom, *Leviticus 1–16* (AB 3; New York, N.Y.: Doubleday, 1991), 150–53. For the terminology in the individual passages, see the chart in Bernd Janowski, *Sühne als Heilsgeschehen: Studien zur Sühnetheologie der Priesterschrift und zur Wurzel KPR im Alten Orient und im Alten Testament* (WMANT 55; Neukirchen-Vluyn: Neukirchener Verlag, 1982), 200.

6. Daube, *New Testament and Rabbinic Judaism*, 232.

7. Ibid., 227. The versional tradition is not of one mind on how many hands Moses laid on Joshua. According to the Masoretic text (MT) of Num 27:18, God tells Moses to "lay your *hand* on him" (singular), while 27:23 relates that Moses "laid his *hands* on him" (plural). Other textual traditions, however, do not contain a disagreement between vv. 18 and 23, although they do not agree with each other: the Samaritan and Syriac traditions use the singular for "hand" in both verses, while the Septuagint uses the plural (τὰς χεῖρας) for "hand" in both verses. (Most inexplicable of all is the rendering of the Luther Bible [1984 edition], in which v. 18 contains a plural form, while v. 23 contains a singular!) John William Wevers doubts that the difference between LXX and MT Num 27:18 is text-critical in origin, "since throughout the Pentateuch the number of יד with suffix is not observed strictly by the translators" (*Notes on the Greek Text of Numbers* [SBLSCS 46; Atlanta, Ga.: Scholars Press, 1998], 466). The principle of *lectio difficilior* probably favors the Masoretic text. So we are left with the question: Is MT 27:18 more correct in its use of the form ידך, or is MT 27:23 more correct with the obviously plural ידיו? René Péter ("L'Imposition des mains dans l'Ancien Testament," *VT* 27 [1977]: 48–55, esp. 50–51) and Janowski (*Sühne als Heilsgeschehen*, 199) argue that the consonantal form in MT 27:18 is *not* singular (as the Masoretic pointers assumed), but rather a defective form of the duel. This seems to be the best solution to the problem. The question of how many hands were used will remain significant throughout our investigation.

there is an equivalence (on some level) in what these hand-laying rites supposedly effect. This typology replaces an earlier one in which the idea of a real transfer was given far less scope. (Daube specifically takes issue with Robertson Smith's claim that the scapegoat ceremony was the only ceremony in which any sort of real transfer took place.)[8] This hand-laying for a real *transfer* contrasts with another category of hand-laying, the act of blessing, in which the hand-layer merely touched his/her hands upon the rite's recipient. The operative concept in the latter is *identification*—the hand-layer is identifying with the one whom he/she is blessing. Daube writes that "[e]vidently" the "physical attitude[s]" of these two categories of hand-laying rites are quite different, and he laments the fact that Greek and English versions of the OT obscure the difference between the type of action denoted by *samakh*, on the one hand, and that denoted by *shim* or *shith*, on the other hand.[9] Daube believes the difference between the two verbs is significant: "In view of the striking external difference between *samakh*, 'leaning of the hands' and *śim* or *shith*, 'a placing of the hands', it would be odd if the two rites had had the same meaning":[10]

> The upshot is that we must keep apart two different kinds of laying on of hands: (1) that which is described by the word *samakh*, (2) that which is described by either of the words *śim* or *shith*. The first kind of imposition is applied to certain offerings, to Levites at their consecration (which was in the nature of an offering by the people), to Joshua at his ordination by Moses and to a criminal convicted of a capital offence. It indicates, we suggest, the pouring of one's personality into another being, the creation of a representative or substitute. It is for this kind of imposition of hands that we propose to use the term *samakh*. The second kind of imposition is applied in blessing and, to some extent, in healing. It indicates the transference of something other than, or less than, the personality; it means the employment of a special, supernatural faculty of one's hands. For this kind of imposition of hands we propose to use the words *śim* and *shith*.[11]

Daube's theory has been very influential within the discussion, but I suggest that it has been given more credence than it deserves. In an article on "Laying On of Hands in the Old Testament," M. C. Sanson shows that Daube's use of the verb *samakh* as a distinguishing mark of a transfer rite is not the skeleton key that Daube

---

8. Daube, *New Testament and Rabbinic Judaism*, 224.

9. Ibid., 227.

10. Ibid., 228.

11. Ibid., 229.

supposes it to be. Noting that peace, sin and burnt offerings are all described with the verb *samakh*, Sanson writes, "The burnt offering and peace offering are not sacrifices concerned with sin; they are more in the nature of gifts of love. Why . . . should we suppose that the laying on of hands is intended to signify the transference of sin?"[12] To understand hand-laying in the case of sacrifice as a real transfer of sin to the animal to be sacrificed, as implied by Daube's interpretation of the use of the verb *samakh*, also poses a difficulty—Sanson writes, "It is [Roland] de Vaux who . . . suggests that if the hand-laying during the sacrifices were intended to mean the transference of sin or guilt, it would then become impossible to burn them as sacrifices, because they would by then be unclean."[13] Sanson's alternative interpretation of the role of hand-laying in the peace, sin and burnt offerings is much to be preferred: "[T]he meaning of the hand-laying is not transference but an attestation (as much to the priest as to God) that the victim comes from this particular individual or group, that it is offered in his or their name, and that the fruit shall be his."[14]

Daube's claim that *samakh* and *shim/shith* represent two very different "physical attitude[s]" has also been challenged. As Wright notes, "[T]his distinction in the form [of the respective gestures] is hard to sustain on the meager evidence. The verb *sāmak* in the Priestly writings may be only idiomatic and not indicate that pressure was applied."[15] The correctness of Wright's suggestion depends on whether one allows the rabbinic discussions of the meaning of *samakh* in sacrificial contexts to carry any weight. Milgrom, who uses the Rabbis as a general key to Leviticus, highlights the fact that the Rabbis invested the term with the same notion of a "physical attitude"

---

12. M. C. Sanson, "Laying On of Hands in the Old Testament," *ExpT* 94 (1983): 323–26 (324). To be sure, Daube spoke of a transfer of "personality," but that poses a problem of its own. As David P. Wright writes, understanding laying hands on a sacrifice to denote a transfer of sorts "do[es] not explain the lack of the gesture with birds and cereal offerings" ("Hands, Laying on of [Old Testament]," in *ABD* 3:47–48 (47). On the sufficiency of carrying small sacrificial animals as an equivalent to identificational hand-laying, see Milgrom, *Leviticus 1–16*, 151–52.

13. Sanson, "Laying On of Hands in the Old Testament," 325.

14. Ibid., 325. It is unfortunate that Sanson feels a need to qualify his position with regard to Moses' ordination of Joshua: he thinks that the fact that Joshua is already a spirit-gifted leader in Num 27 means that his ordination at the hands of Moses represented, not a transfer of the "Spirit of wisdom," but rather one of "authority" (325). This is an unfortunate reading of the biblical evidence. For one thing, a transfer of authority sounds too similar to the *other* type of hand-laying rite. For another thing, the transfer of an unction associated with a particular task is hardly incompatible with the notion that the one receiving that unction was already Spirit-filled—a point easily proved from the NT! For the laying on of hands in the OT, see Janowski, *Sühne als Heilsgeschehen*, 199–205, and the studies cited there at p. 199 (n. 80).

15. Wright, "Hands," (n. 12), 47.

[Daube's term] that Daube had ascribed to it.[16] But does that mean that the Rabbis independently attest to the correctness of Daube's rendering? Hardly—Daube himself appears to have taken his view of the meaning of *samakh* from the Rabbis.[17]

Daube's attempt to use these two categories of hand-laying rites as a lens on ritual activity in the NT is also far from compelling. He is undoubtedly correct to oppose one type of hand-laying to another, but the way in which he identifies a given NT rite as an example of *samakh* over against *shim/shith* (or vice versa) is usually open to doubt. One wonders, for example, why Daube thinks that the laying of hands upon the deacons in Acts 6:6 is an example of *samakh*. (Daube translates the Greek, rather tendentiously, as "they 'leaned their hands on them.'") Daube takes the rite in question to be of the "real transfer" variety, yet he interprets it as one in which the apostles appointed "representatives" (in the sense of "extended selves"), and he even refers to the deacons' task of distributing charity as "the community living in its deputies."[18] If the object of the rite is to appoint representatives or deputies, should we not expect the rite to be of the more symbolic variety, *viz*. the one denoted in Hebrew by *shim* or *shith*? Daube gives no explanation for his odd interpretation. He even highlights the fact that it is the *people* who laid hands on the elders: "It might perhaps be objected that, when first proposing the scheme, the apostles speak of men 'whom we may appoint over this business.' But 'we' here most probably includes those whom they address; it means 'we, the Christians of Jerusalem', not 'we, the apostles.'"[19]

I am puzzled that Daube would say that the *people* "lean[ed]" their hands on the deacons, in order to make them "into their representatives": as I argue below, when the community is directly involved with the hand-laying rite, it is *not* a rite of real transfer, but rather the (quite separate) rite of identification or representation. Jerome Quinn and William Wacker also note that Daube's identification of the laying on of hands for healing as an instance of *shim/shith* conflicts with the language of the Qumranic *Genesis Apocryphon*: "the healing *epithesis* of the Gospels and Acts

---

16. Milgrom, *Leviticus 1–16*, 150.

17. There is something risky about letting rabbinic definitions of terms serve as a lens for interpreting those terms in OT context. This is especially true when the Rabbis put those definitions front and center within their discussions, and when they turn the supposed distinctions between terms into a principal of exegesis.

18. Daube, *New Testament and Rabbinic Judaism*, 237.

19. Ibid., 238.

ought to have corresponded in the *Sitz im Leben Jesu* to the *sāmak* of 1QapGen."[20] (That Jesus' healings involve a transfer of sorts is suggested by Mark 5:30 // Luke 8:46.)[21] Part of the reason for Daube's confusion may lie in his unfortunate choice of the word "personality" in his description of what is transferred in the hand-*leaning* rite. It is not one's personality, but rather an unction (easily separable from one's personality), which, in the language of *Numbers Rabba*, is "poured from vessel to vessel."[22] Daube's misstep in this regard provides the only logical explanation that I can imagine for why he would identify a communal hand-laying rite with a rite of transfer.

I wish to suggest a more reliable approach than that of second-guessing which Hebrew verb corresponds best to a given hand-laying rite in the NT. Sanson notes a different distinction between the various OT hand-laying rites: the text refers to the laying of a *hand* (singular) rather than *hands* (plural) on the sacrificial victim, but both hands are employed in other hand-laying rites. Sanson notes that peace, sin and burnt offerings all have the use of a single hand in common, but in the scapegoat ceremony, Aaron lays *both* hands on the head of the animal (Lev 16:21).[23] Sanson speaks rather reservedly about using the one-/two-hand distinction as a key to unlocking the meaning of every rite: "It is just conceivable," he writes, "that [the two types of hand-laying rites] may correspond to the use of two hands or one." He correctly notes that it is impossible to tell, in some cases, how many hands are

---

20. Jerome D. Quinn and William C. Wacker, *The First and Second Letters to Timothy* (Eerdmans Critical Commentary; Grand Rapids, Mich.: Eerdmans, 2000), 393. For another critique of Daube's extension of his hand-*leaning* theory to NT practices, see J. K. Parratt, "The Laying on of Hands in the New Testament: A Re-examination in the Light of the Hebrew Terminology," *ExpT* 80 (1968-69): 210-14.

21. Ceslas Spicq, commenting on 1 Tim 4:14, writes, "L'imposition des mains, transmettant une puissance divine, était le geste du aître pour rendre la santé aux malades (*Mc.* v, 23; vi, 5; vii, 33; viii, 23, 25; *Lc.* iv, 40; xiii, 13)" (*Les Épitres Pastorales* [Études bibliques; Paris: Gabalda, 41969], 517).

22. It is unfortunate that so many commentaries on the Pastoral Epistles uncritically adopt Daube's typology—e.g., I. Howard Marshall, *A Critical and Exegetical Commentary on the Pastoral Epistles* (ICC; Edinburgh: T & T Clark, 1999), 567.

23. Sanson, "Laying On of Hands in the Old Testament," 324. Wright assumes that all hand-laying rites not connected with sacrifice involve the placement of two hands rather than one ("Hands," 48). He therefore assumes that the guilt-signifying ritual of Leviticus 24 involves two hands, although the text is unclear. The significance of one hand versus two hands would later be emphasized by Péter, "L'Imposition des mains dans l'Ancien Testament" (n. 7), 54–55. In light of the apparent importance of the number of hands involved in a given rite, it is unfortunate that some modern redescriptions of these rites are sometimes careless in reporting this matter. E.g., Roland de Vaux switches back and forth between "hand" and "hands" in his description of a burnt sacrifice (*Ancient Israel: Religious Institutions* [New York: McGraw-Hill, 1965], 2:415–16).

involved in a given rite, and he cautions that "it is only a desire for neatness that demands that all the uses [of the hand-laying gesture] should be subsumed under one head."[24] Yet a test fit of his suggestion, in both OT and NT contexts, suggests that he is on to something very significant.

Laying On of Hands in the New Testament

The book of Acts presents what is presumably a one-hand rite of hand-laying in Acts 6, where the community ordains a number of deacons for the purpose of lessening the apostles' workload. We have already seen how Daube interprets this rite: he believes that it involves a transfer of the community's "personality" to the newly ordained deacons, a transfer which installs or outfits them to be the community's representatives in some sense. Most scholars read this passage in a less problematic way: the rite did *not* convey any sort of personality transfer, but rather, by way of an identificational gesture (equivalent to that used in the OT for peace, sin and burnt offerings), it signified that the deacons represented the community. There is no mention of any sort of endowment with a special unction. Thornton, observing that in Acts 6 Luke describes Stephen as a man "full of faith and the Holy Ghost" (v. 5), surmises that Luke "followed carefully the model set for him in the scriptural statements about Joshua" (see Deut 34:9).[25] But even if the echo is a true one (which can hardly be granted so readily), we should not deduce from it that the hand-laying rite in v. 6 was of the same variety as Moses' laying of hands upon Joshua. Stephen's qualifications are mentioned for the sake of the episode immediately following the ordination (where he is again described as being "full of grace and power" [v. 8]), an episode materially separate from the narrative of the deacons' ordination. In all likelihood, this hand-laying should *not* be compared with Moses' passing of the mantle to Joshua. It has more in common with the laying of hands on the Levites (Num 8:10).

The association of a two-hand rite with a real transfer of power or unction appears in Acts, in connection with imparting the Spirit to believers (8:17–19; 9:17; 19:6). Here is the clearest case, of course, of a real transfer through the act of laying hands on someone. Although Acts also indicates that the Spirit could be given without the laying on of hands (as in the case of Cornelius' household [10:1–48], see

---

24. Sanson, "Laying On of Hands in the Old Testament," 326.

25. Lionel S. Thornton, *Confirmation: Its Place in the Baptismal Mystery* (Westminster, London: Dacre, 1954), 77. Quinn and Wacker also believe that a conscious echo of Moses' laying of hands on Joshua is intended (*First and Second Letters to Timothy*, 398).

too 8:16). These examples and precedents of Spirit-reception establish an apostolic tradition.

Admittedly, there is one place in the NT where the one-hand/two-hand distinction breaks down: the gospel accounts of Jesus' healing ministry. In several places, Jesus *touches* or *lays* (or is asked to lay) a single hand on the one being healed or blessed (Matt 8:3 // Mark 1:41 // Luke 5:13; Matt 8:15 [Mark 1:31 has it that he simply "took her by the hand", while in Luke 8:39 he rebukes the fever without touching her]; 9:18 [in v. 25, he takes the archon's daughter by the hand]; Mark 7:32).[26] How we count this evidence depends on whether "touching" is the same as "laying hands on." In a majority of instances, Jesus lays two hands on the one being healed or blessed (Matt 19:13, 15; Mark 5:23; 6:5; 8:23, 25; 10:16; 14:46; 16:18; Luke 4:40; 13:13), and in the (secondary) ending to Mark, Jesus promises that those who believe "shall lay hands on the sick and they shall recover" (16:18). Likewise, Paul lays two hands on Publius' father in Acts 28:8. In Acts 9, the textual tradition exhibits some variation as to the number of hands Ananias *should* have used in ministering healing and the reception of the gift of the Holy Spirit: in Paul's vision (v. 12), Ananias lays a single hand on him in one significant textual unit and both hands in two other textual units,[27] while in the fulfillment of that vision (v. 17), Ananias uses both hands (v. 17).

Obviously, if healing involves the impartation of a healing power (δύναμις) from one party to another,[28] then we should expect the two-handed approach to

---

26. Quinn and Wacker, *First and Second Letters to Timothy*, 392–93.

27. C. K. Barrett, *Acts* (ICC; Edinburgh: T & T Clark, 1994), 1:454, briefly notes that at 9:12 there is "strong evidence for the omission of τάς, also for the singular χεῖρα." He thinks, however, that τὰς χεῖρας (ℵ^c B E) is "probably correct." {The 27th edition of Nestle-Aland decides for the long reading with τὰς χεῖρας (ℵ^c B E). Kurt Aland is known to give Vaticanus strong weight because of its agreement with P75 and here there is also then an immediate agreement with τὰς χεῖρας at 9:17. This decision is a change from the 25th edition that opted for χεῖρας with the omission of τὰς (following P74vid ℵ* A C). The omission of τὰς is certainly striking. Perhaps the most difficult reading to account for as a scribal emendation, which carries some weight here towards duplicating the original script, is the singular χεῖρα which is attested by Ψ 33 M (= Majority text, including the Byzantine Koine text) it vg^{mss} sy. One might speculate that the first hand of Sinaiticus added a final sigma to the singular form in his precursor at 9:12 to harmonize with 9:17, but did not want to insert the article as well, which was then the added by a corrector. Scenarios accounting for the three textual units are illusive with the manuscript evidence available. Therefore, the least speculative course overall is to regard the weight of ℵ^c B E (τὰς χεῖρα) at 9:12 as probably offering the best solution. Interestingly, in light of Luke 5:13 (χεῖρα) and Acts 6:6; 9:17 (τὰς χεῖρας), all three textual variants (χεῖρα, χεῖρας, and τὰς χεῖρας) imply that Luke did not recognize a phenomenological distinction between one hand and two. This is consistent with Poirier's argument here.} — Ed.

28. Cf. James D. G. Dunn: "No doubt a flow of energy from healer to healed was actually experi-

predominate (which it does)—but what shall we do with the exceptions? Source criticism will take us part of the way, as the Markan parallel to Matt 9:18 testifies to a greater presence of two-handed healings in the earlier form of the tradition. Differentiating between *touching* and *laying hands on* someone also accounts for some of the difference—the verb ἅπτω is used in Matt 8:3 // Mark 1:41 // Luke 5:13, and in Matt 8:15. Matthew's omission of any reference to Jesus feeling "power" go out from him when the woman touched his clothes/hem/fringe (as detailed in Mark 5:30 // Luke 8:46) suggests that Matthew may have viewed Jesus' healings as happening on a wholly different plain from those effected by the disciples, and it may be that Matthew did not feel constrained to have Jesus use two hands. This is only a surmise, but it fits with Matthew's change of "his clothes" (as found in Mark 5:28, 30) to "the hem of his garment" (9:20), as well as his recycling of this healing by hem-touching in 14:36. If we confine ourselves to the Markan text, *and* if we ignore references to *touching* rather than *laying* hands, there is only one instance in which Jesus lays or is asked to lay a single hand in order to effect a cure: Mark 7:32, where the people beg him to "lay his hand" on a deaf man.[29] The use of two hands in the practice of laying on hands for healing is thus more strongly attested in the gospels than the use of one hand.

The Pastoral Epistles

What then can we say about 1 Tim 4:14 and 2 Tim 1:6? By all appearances, 1 Tim 4:14 refers to an act of ordination, and *not* to an act of unction transfer, which is something altogether different. By "ordination", however, I mean something very different from what Daube meant. I mean that it refers to an act by which the community (through the elders) showed its approval of Timothy by identifying him as their representative—that they were vouching for his fitness for ministry and/or

---

enced in many cases through the physical contact (cf. Mark 5.28f. pars.), though whether the energy was thereby simply released from the latent resources of one or other, or channelled through the man of faith to the sick person from sources outside of himself (God/risen Jesus) we cannot at this distance even begin to judge" (*Jesus and the Spirit: A Study of the Religious and Charismatic Experience of Jesus and the First Christians as Reflected in the New Testament* [London: SCM, 1975], 165).

29. It bears mentioning that the healing of Pharaoh in the *Genesis Apocryphon* is effected by the laying on of *two* hands. David Flusser writes, "the Genesis Apocryphon tells us what we could have assumed, namely, that Jesus was not the first to heal by the laying-on of hands, and that this practice was current in some Jewish circles" (*Judaism and the Origins of Christianity* [Jerusalem: Magnes, 1988], 22). If this rite *was* current in Judaism, then presumably it was current in the same form as in the Qumranic text (*viz.* as a two-hand rite).

his calling. To be ordained, then, means to have the local church's seal of approval. Ideally, the candidate will also have God's approval, but, ritually speaking, the rite does not *directly* signify that at all. Of course, in the case of 1 Timothy, we know that God approved Timothy for the ministry to which he was ordained, as God's will was revealed in that case by prophecy. The "laying on of the hands of the presbytery" most likely involved the laying of a single hand on the part of each elder, as the parallel with similar rites elsewhere suggests. By contrast, 2 Tim 1:6 refers to Paul laying *two* hands on Timothy. The rite in 2 Timothy, therefore, would appear to be quite different from that in 1 Timothy. Paul's two-hand rite represented a direct transfer, to Timothy, of something residing in Paul.

There is nothing new, of course, about my interpretation of these two verses, other than (perhaps) my application of Sanson's typology. But confusion still reigns in the commentaries, much of it caused by Daube's mistaken identification of ordinational hand-laying as a gesture of transfer. Sanson's typology, I suggest, draws the proper distinction between ordination and unction transfer. Those who have arrived at the same understanding of 1 Tim 4:14 and 2 Tim 1:6 as I have, often have done so on the basis of the prepositions used in these verses:

> 1 Tim 4:14, "Do not neglect the gift that is in you, which was given to you through (διά) prophecy with (μετά) the laying on of hands by the council of elders."

> 2 Tim 1:6, "For this reason I remind you to rekindle the gift of God that is within you through (διά) the laying on of my hands."

A number of scholars have drawn attention to the fact that "the laying on of hands" (ἐπιθέσεως τῶν χειρῶν) is preceded by μετά in 1 Tim 4:14, and by διά in 2 Tim 1:6. The difference is telling—as C. K. Barrett notes, the laying on of hands in 1 Tim 4:14 is "not a means" but rather "an accompanying act" for the endowment on Timothy of a charism, for "μετά with the genitive must mean 'with,' not 'through.'"[30] The language of 1 Tim 4:14, of course, does indicate a certain giving of a gift "through" something, but the giving comes through *prophecy* rather than through

---

30. C. K. Barrett, *The Pastoral Epistles* (NCB; Oxford: Clarendon, 1963), 71–72. See the excursus on "διά und μετά in I Tim 4, 14 und II Tim 1, 6" in Hermann von Lips, *Glaube – Gemeinde – Amt: Zum Verständnis der Ordination in den Pastoralbriefen* (FRLANT 122; Göttingen: Vandenhoeck & Ruprecht, 1979), 250–53. Gordon D. Fee similarly notes, "the preposition μετά has no known instance in the Koine of an instrumental sense" (*God's Empowering Presence: The Holy Spirit in the Letters of Paul* [Peabody, Ma.: Hendrickson, 1994], 775).

the laying on of hands.³¹ Philology cannot carry the whole argument, however, as the sense of "through" conveyed by διά might well be a weak sense, practically implying accompaniment as well.³² The difference between the prepositions alerts us to the potential difference between these two hand-laying rites, but the real substance of the argument lies elsewhere.

What does our decision to follow Sanson's typology of hand-laying rites have to offer in the case of 1 and 2 Timothy? It makes all the difference in our understanding of 1 Tim 4:14 and 2 Tim 1:6 if we adopt Sanson's typology over against Daube's much more widely used typology. Consider the effect of K. Grayston's attempt to apply Daube's distinction between "placing" and "pressing" hands to the NT.³³ He connects "placing of hands" with healings throughout the gospels and Acts, and with conferring the Holy Spirit in Acts 8:17–19; 9:12, 17; 19:6; and Heb 6:2, but he connects "pressing of hands" with the appointment of the seven in Acts 6:6, and with the sending of Paul and Barnabas in Acts 13:3. Both of these gestures, he thinks, can "perhaps" be found in 1 Tim 4:14 and 2 Tim 1:6:

> These passages combine both sorts of imposition: that which conveys the gift and that which conveys identity. The distinction between *sim-shith* and *samakh* may have been maintained while the Church mainly drew its inspiration from Jewish Christianity, but it was early lost among Gentile Christians—especially as LXX and New Testament writers represented both sorts of expression by ἐπίθεσις τῶν χειρῶν. One consequence of this amalgamation is that the imposition of hands by itself does not convey a clear and definite meaning. It became a recognized principle in the later Church that the meaning can be discerned only in the prayer by which the imposition is accompanied or by the explicit intention with which it is administered.³⁴

---

31. Cf. Benjamin Fiore: "Here [in 1 Tim 4:14] the preposition *dia* ('through') indicates that the prophecy was effective in the transmission of the charism and task to Timothy, although the imposition of hands appears to be an 'accompanying' (*meta*) act rather than an effective gesture as it is at 2 Tim 1:6" (*The Pastoral Epistles: First Timothy, Second Timothy, Titus* [SP 12; Collegeville, Minn.: Liturgical, 2007], 96). See esp. Spicq, *Épitres Pastorales*, 516–17.

32. See Marshall, *Critical and Exegetical Commentary on the Pastoral Epistles*, 567.

33. K. Grayston, "The Significance of the Word *Hand* in the New Testament," in *Mélanges bibliques en hommage au R. P. Béda Rigaux* (ed. Albert Descamps and André de Halleux; Gembloux: Duculot, 1970), 479–87.

34. Ibid., 487.

Grayston may be appealing too hurriedly to a loss of the rite's original form—on the terms of Sanson's typology, no such loss has occurred. The "laying on of hands of the presbytery" (1 Tim 4:14) would most likely involve the laying on of a *single* hand by each elder—that is, if the pattern of communal hand-laying found in the OT is relevant—while Paul's hand-laying (2 Tim 1:6) explicitly involves both hands.

What is Meant by "Transfer"?

The above discussion brings a further question to bear: In what way is there a transfer of unction from Paul to Timothy in 2 Tim 1:6? Is the transfer really as material as the term "transfer" implies? That is, did the author of 2 Timothy really believe that something pneumatic could have flowed through Paul's arms to Timothy? Or does an understanding of what really happens on a pneumatological level involve a demythologizing of the gesture of transfer? In other words, does God merely create the impression of a transfer by honoring the gesture with an independent impartation of an equivalent unction?[35]

Most commentators seem to assume that a materialist model is too crude and anthropocentric to represent what happens in the hand-laying rite. For example, Parratt writes, in connection with the laying on of apostolic hands in Acts 8:17 and 19:6,

> [T]his [spirit-filling] clearly was not regarded as taking place in any purely mechanical way.... The laying on of hands can perhaps ... be best understood as the outward accompaniment of the intercessory prayer offered by the apostle on behalf of the new convert. It signifies in an outward form the act of blessing, and is not directly connected with the physical transference of power.[36]

One wonders how Parratt can see this so "clearly." Where is the evidence? The light that makes this clear for him comes from somewhere other than Scripture—and

---

35. The Protestant penchant for the latter may lie behind Wright's demythologizing of the hand-laying rites in Lev 16:21 and Num 27:23: "In Leviticus 16 Aaron demonstrates what object is the recipient of the sins of the people. The rite here is not strictly a means of transfer; sins do not travel through Aaron's arms to the goat. It merely points out where the sins confessed by Aaron are to alight.... In Numbers 27 the rite demonstrates who Moses' successor will be. Again here, in view of the preceding examples, authority is not passed through Moses' arms to Joshua. Moses by the gesture merely points out who the recipient of his authority is and demonstrates to the community that Joshua is his legal successor" ("Hands," 48). I find no hint in Scripture that these rites should be demythologized in such a way.

36. Parratt "Laying on of Hands" (n. 20), 214.

probably from a time much later than Scripture. If we apply Sanson's typology, we can see *more* clearly that the hand-laying act in question is *not* the act of blessing (which is a one-handed act). Raymond Collins is similarly offended by the materialist model, and attempts to head off a more literal interpretation of the preposition in 2 Tim 1:6: "The causal connotations of 'through' should not be exaggerated. At most, 'through' suggests God's chosen instrument; minimally, it might only suggest that the gift was given during the ritual gesture."[37] Collins does not spell out why the "most" that he will allow must fall so short of the literal meaning of the passage.[38]

Part of the reason for this assumption on the part of commentators, undoubtedly, lies in the Protestant bias against crediting human agency or initiative for supernatural effects. When a modern evangelist with a healing ministry is claimed to have "healed" someone, most Protestants instinctively cry out against such "careless" language: Only *God* heals, they claim, and crediting a mere evangelist with a healing is to rob God of glory. But this approach ignores the plain language of the book of Acts: although most references to healing in Acts are expressed in the divine passive, we are told, in Acts 28:8, that "Paul" healed Publius' father. Of course, no reader, ancient or modern, supposes that Paul healed someone by his *own* power, and no one would think that Paul (or the modern healing evangelist) would be daft enough to think that he did so, but that is beside the point. Scripture does not wince where Protestant sensibilities wince—the NT speaks of supernatural workings (including healings, prophesyings, etc.) as the effects of human initiative, even though it is the Spirit of God who causes all these things to happen. In some way, apparently, God

---

37. Raymond F. Collins, *1 & 2 Timothy and Titus: A Commentary* (NTL; Louisville: Westminster John Knox, 2002), 130 (his n. 65).

38. Frances Young confuses the issue along different lines when she asks, with reference to all three hand-laying references in 1 and 2 Timothy, whether the Spirit "[i]s . . . channelled through the bearers of the tradition," and decides against this scenario on the grounds that one of the three references (she thinks) "refers to renewal in baptism," which "must apply to all baptised believers who are faithful to the teaching" (*The Theology of the Pastoral Letters* [New Testament Theology; Cambridge: Cambridge University Press, 1994], 69–70). Unfortunately, Young does not make it clear which of the three references supposedly "refers to renewal in baptism" (the best guess is that Young has in mind the language of "rekindle the gift of God that is within you" [2 Tim 1:6]), and she compounds this by connecting this (still hidden) reference with a quotation that the unsuspecting reader would assume to be lifted from the context of the passage in question, but which in fact comes from a different letter altogether (Tit 3:6). Young nowhere tells the reader the source of that quotation or what its connection with one of the hand-laying references in 1 or 2 Timothy is purported to be. The effect of Young's cut-and-paste job is that 2 Tim 1:6 is made to look like a reference to the laying on of hands in connection with water baptism. While it is possible that this is what 2 Tim 1:6 is really about, it is hardly as likely as Young presents it.

allows the Spirit to be brokered (within limits) by the ministers of the Church—although the NT emphasizes that such control is safeguarded from corrupt motives and non-apostolic channels.[39]

This brings us to the recent debate between Friedrich Wilhelm Horn and Volker Rabens regarding the notion of the divine Spirit as *Stoff*. Horn argued that, at an early stage of the NT (and its predecessor traditions within second-temple Judaism), the Spirit had been conceptualized as a material of sorts, not unlike the Stoic concept of the materialization of πνεῦμα.[40] While reacting against some of the more fanciful elements in Horn's developmental history, Rabens took issue with Horn's claim that the Spirit was thought of in material terms. According to Rabens, those NT passages that sound like they conceive of the Spirit in material terms are purely metaphorical: "With metaphors like 'poured out' Jewish (and Christian) writers do not . . . intend to convey insights about the nature of the Holy Spirit; rather, they are a means of reference to a (new) nexus of the Spirit's activities in the persons concerned."[41] Rabens argues convincingly, in my opinion, that this language about the Spirit *could be* metaphorical, but I do not think he has shown that it *must* be metaphorical through and through. Horn's developmental scheme would probably crumble under the weight of its own detail—Horn turns every little hint of difference between writers into a matter of development in the history of the idea of *pneuma*—but it is *not* the necessary alternative to Rabens's purely anti-materialist scheme. Rabens takes issue with a literal interpretation of materialist language about the Spirit (e.g., the image of God "pouring out" the Spirit), but there are also the hand-laying rites that reinforce this language to some degree, and it is also possible to view the language of "pouring out" as a metaphor while yet holding to the concept of a more literal pouring that takes place in hand-laying rites. Is there any compelling reason to dismiss the extension of

---

39. Susan R. Garrett correctly notes, with respect to Luke-Acts, that the divine agent is never far from the narrative's view (*The Demise of the Devil: Magic and the Demonic in Luke's Writings* [Minneapolis, Minn.: Fortress, 1989], 66).

40. Horn writes, "Der Geist repräsentiert Gott im Menschen, ja der Mensch hat Teil am göttlichen πνεῦμα (Seneca, *Ep* 41,2). Hier ist die von Aristoteles aufrecht erhaltene Unterscheidung von πνεῦμα und νοῦς wieder aufgegeben. Es kommt zu einer 'Materialisation des Geistes'. Die Übertragung des Geistes bedarf verschiedener Hilfsstoffe, an die sich das πνεῦμα stofflich bindet (Wasser, Öl, Speisen etc). In der Stoa schließlich ist eine Identifizierung von Geist und Gott belegt (Chrysipp, frg 310.913 u.o.)" (*Das Angeld des Geistes: Studien zur paulinischen Pneumatologie* [FRLANT 154; Göttingen: Vandenhoeck & Ruprecht, 1992], 57).

41. Volker Rabens, "The Develpoment of Pauline Pneumatology: A Response to F. W. Horn," *BZ* 43 (1999): 161–79 (171).

this materialist imagery into ritual as nothing more than an overactive metaphor? At what point do we consider that language might be more than metaphorical?

It may be that we are trying to peer beyond God's attempt to meet us within the limitations of our language and our world of conceptual possibilities. As Rabens notes, "[E]ven if the Spirit were imparted by the sacraments this would still allow for a functional, substantial *or* material conception of the Spirit."[42] My point, however, is that those who conducted the hand-laying rites in Scripture assumed that the Spirit (or sin, or unction, or impurity, etc.) was really transmitted *through* the act of laying hands on someone or something, and that neither onlookers nor participants were intended to demythologize that rite.[43]

Conclusion

In spite of its popularity, Daube's attempt to use the rabbinic distinction between *samakh* and *shim/shith* as the basis for a typology of hand-laying rites really has little going for it. A better typology is provided by the simple distinction between the number of hands normally employed in these rites—a distinction noted by Sanson, Péter, and others. The real test of the latter typology lies in its application to the NT examples of hand-laying rites. As I have tried to argue, it passes that test in near-perfect form. In the case of 1 and 2 Timothy, this distinction seems to indicate that the laying on of the elders' hands in 1 Tim 4:14 and the laying on of Paul's hands in 2 Tim 1:6 are very different things—the former is an identificational rite ("ordination"), while the latter involves a real transfer of a charism from Paul to Timothy.

It has not been my intention to argue a hard-line position on this matter. My purpose here is merely to field an option that no one else (as far as I can see) has given due consideration. Many people apparently recoil at the suggestion that the Spirit could be conveyed in almost fluid terms, supposing it to be incompatible with the idea of the Spirit as a *person*.[44] But I suggest that there really is no reason that the

---

42. Ibid., 171.

43. The similarity between prayer for Spirit-baptism and prayer with laying on of hands for healing is another reason we should be cautious about dismissing the fluidity of the Spirit too quickly: the way in which divine healing power is transmitted often parallels established Jewish understandings of impurity egress. (See Acts 5:15, in which Peter's shadow apparently spreads healing power in way that recalls how the "overhang" spreads impurity.) If we reason that the Spirit simply cannot be transmitted in such a "fluid" way, should not Scripture's description of how the power of divine healing works fall under the same stricture?

44. I. Howard Marshall has written that "[t]he language of persons, as applied to God, is analogical" ("Incarnational Christology in the New Testament," in *Christ the Lord: Studies in Christology Presented*

Spirit could not be both fluid (at least *functionally*) *and* a person. When the Bible conceives of a divine unction, it thinks of that unction as distinct from other unctions, but also, *at the same time*, as the personal presence of the Spirit of God. How is that possible? The answer is that we do not know, but *that* (*viz.* our not knowing) is in keeping with many ontological questions about God. If the Spirit, on the day of Pentecost, could enter a room as a "mighty rushing wind" and yet still be God in person, why could not that same Spirit flow like an electric charge or a divine fluid from one person to another? Interpreters have tended to ride roughshod over the possibilities.

---

to Donald Guthrie [ed. Harold H. Rowdon; Leicester: InterVarsity, 1982], 1–16 (3 [n. 6]). This claim strikes me as odd, as I have always thought of a "person" as a "thinking, living subjectivity," so that the personhood of God is one of the aspects of divinity that is not too lofty for us to understand in a more direct way. Nick Norelli has suggested to me that Marshall thinks of the term "person" quite differently—that he uses it as a near synonym for "human being."

Mikeal C. Parsons, *Luke: Storyteller, Interpreter, Evangelist*

REVIEWED BY ROB STARNER

rstarner@sagu.edu
Southwestern Assemblies of God University, Waxahachie, Texas 75165

From the pen of NT scholar and narrative critic Mikeal Parsons,[1] readers may experience what the author refers to as a "series of *forays* into the Lukan *terrain*."[2] For any who mistakenly access an "attack" schema for the term "foray" and on that account expect a skeptical approach to the Lukan corpus, the author's discussion on "the Making of 'Luke'" in the first chapter of the book gives that notion a fitting and proper burial. Parsons' apparent confidence in the historical trustworthiness of Luke-Acts is refreshing in light of the practice of many literary critics who approach their task with little or no concern for historical referentiality.[3] While some see the bridle of historical referentiality as an unwelcome impediment to what Johnson has fittingly labeled "flights of fancy,"[4] others argue that to esteem the contribution that knowledge of real (i.e., flesh-and-blood) authors, real (i.e., original) readers, and surrounding historical circumstances makes to interpreting documents and, indeed, to rightly understanding their rhetorical function is a mark of sound judgment and sober historiography.[5] Thankfully, Parsons' work is not undercut by any hopelessly naïve notions of the autonomy of the text.

---

1. Mikeal C. Parsons, *Luke: Storyteller, Interpreter, Evangelist* (Peabody, Mass.: Hendrickson, 2007. Pp. xxii + 230. Paper. $19.95. ISBN 978-156563-483-1.

2. Parsons, *Luke*, xi (emphasis his).

3. Critique of this misunderstanding is not a modern novelty. See, for example, Ched Myers (*Binding the Strong Man: A Political Reading of Mark's Story of Jesus* [Maryknoll, N. Y.: Orbis, 1988], 24) who faulted the early literary critics who "try to liberate the text from all historical referentiality whatsoever." Myers' own methodology purposed to combine both historical and literary perspectives, allowing each approach to compensate for the weaknesses of the other.

4. Luke Timothy Johnson, *The Real Jesus: The Misguided Quest for the Historical Jesus and the Truth of the Historical Gospels* (San Francisco, Calif.: Harper Collins, 1996), 100.

5. See, for example, Amos N. Wilder, *The Bible and the Literary Critic* (Minneapolis, Minn.: Fortress, 1991), 29–30) who cautions: "If narrative is ultimately 'intentional' and 'suasive,' this undercuts any

Although none of Parsons' conclusions hangs on the actual identity of Luke, the author nevertheless begins his book with the tradition-based conviction that the author of Luke-Acts was Luke, the "beloved physician" and missionary co-worker of Paul and proceeds to explicate how this understanding has "withstood both the test of time and the critical eye of modern biblical scholarship."[6] In summary fashion the author probes the main lines of this debate and concludes: "Luke the beloved physician emerges as a likely—though, importantly, not the only—candidate."[7] While this phraseology ultimately leaves the question of authorship open-ended, Parsons wraps up the discussion by urging his readers to keep in mind "the *stability* of the tradition that identifies Luke as the author."[8] This caveat is important because the real author, real audience, and actual circumstances are important factors that influence the use of literary techniques, handling of sources, and compositional intentions reflected by the text.

Modern scholarly efforts to establish the historical Luke, while evidently of little need, interest or value in their original setting, are nevertheless hermeneutically advantageous in the contemporary setting. From the outset of his book Parsons notes that some understanding of authorial identity is "prerequisite to considering the writer as a storyteller, interpreter, and evangelist,"[9] although this plays a smaller role in the book than some readers might expect.

Judging from the striking anonymity of each gospel writer, it seems clear that none of the Evangelists felt a sense of "ownership" of the materials he "handed down." None sought to ground the reliability and authority of his story on his identity or position or prominence. None sought personal "credit" or acclaim for the contribution he had made. The degree to which this reflects (1) a self-depreciatory mindset, or (2) a sober acknowledgment of the role of the community in the selection, transmission, and shaping of the gospel materials, or (3) a holy reverence for the Spirit of God who superintended the entire process in such a manner that the final product is precisely what God himself desired is difficult to assay. Particularly striking, however, are the numerous counterexamples found among the extra-biblical historiographers. Compare, for example, Herodotus: "These are the researches of Herodotus

---

strict view of the autonomy of the text. . . . That 'no narrative can be transparent on historical fact' does not mean that all links with our human experience, all resonances, are excluded. The very act of reading involves a correlation of text and life and therefore some prior referentiality of the text."

6. Parsons, *Luke*, 2.

7. Ibid., 8.

8. Ibid., 8 (emphasis his).

9. Ibid., 1.

of Halicarnassus, which he publishes . . ."[10]; Thucydides: "Thucydides, an Athenian, wrote the history of the war between the Peloponnesians and the Athenians . . ."[11]; Pliny the Elder, "C. Plinius Secundus to His Friend Titus Vespasian . . ."[12]; Josephus, ". . . Joseph, the son of Matthias, by birth a Hebrew, a priest also, and one who at first fought against the Romans myself, and was forced to be present at what was done afterwards, [am the author of this work][13]). Luke's refusal to follow suit means that the reception of his work must stand strictly on its own merits, a point that Parsons does not exploit.

When it comes to conclusions regarding the actual identity of the author of any ancient writing, some degree of tentativeness is warranted. To be sure, the answers to nearly all historical inquiries are restricted to "probability" statements. Nevertheless, in spite of the axiomatic nature of this assertion, many strands of historical data have a sufficiently high quality and/or quantity of corroboratory details that historians feel compelled to speak of them as "assured results." Parsons nowhere makes this kind of bald assertion regarding the authorship of Luke-Acts, but he does (perhaps for rhetorical purposes?) leave several important corroboratory strands "hanging" for readers to process. For example, he notes that the title εὐαγγέλιον κατὰ Λουκᾶν "appears at the end of the oldest extant manuscript of the Gospel of Luke" and concludes that identifying this "Luke" as Luke the physician is "a logical inference."[14] We should hasten to note that to date not a single reconstructed hypothesis or alternate explanatory theory has provided a better candidate for authorship—let alone succeeded in overturning the arguments for traditional authorship. Surely this is significant. Thus, the business of conducting exegetical "forays" into the Lukan "terrain" under the assumption of traditional authorship trades minimal methodological risk for potentially substantial exegetical gain.

As the title of the book suggests, but the term "terrain" obfuscates, Parsons arranges his investigations of Luke-Acts under three *author*-centered rubrics: storyteller, interpreter, and evangelist. These studies ostensibly are concerned not so much with the real (i.e., historical) author, but with what scholars can discover about

10. Herodotus, *History, Book 1*, trans. George Rawlinson, http://classics.mit.edu/Herodotus/history.1.i.html (accessed 2/8/09).

11. Thucydides, *The History of the Peloponnesian War, Book 1*, trans. Richard Crawley, http://classics.mit.edu/Thucydides/pelopwar.1.first.html (accessed 2/8/09).

12. Pliny the Elder, *The Natural History*, trans. John Bostock, http://www.perseus.tufts.edu/hopper/text.jsp?doc=Perseus:text:1999.02.0137 (accessed 2/8/09).

13. Josephus, *The Wars of the Jews 1.3*, http://www.perseus.tufts.edu/hopper/text.jsp?doc=Perseus:text:1999.01.0148 (accessed 2/14/09).

14. Parsons, *Luke*, 4.

the real author's literary techniques, handling of sources, and compositional intentions through a careful examination of his work. That is why after discussing in Chapter One the accepted details concerning the historical Luke, Parsons begins his investigation of the literary techniques of Luke in Chapter Two with the thought: "Regardless of the 'true identity' of the author of Luke-Acts . . . ."[15] Yet, equally important—and perhaps more so—are the insights derived from a more thorough understanding of the historical Luke, insofar as this knowledge is accessible.[16]

In addition to engaging modern skepticism regarding the traditional identification of Luke, Parsons also dialogues with what he refers to as a "small but vocal minority" of NT scholars who have recently called into question the timeworn belief in the Gentile ethnicity of both the author and the audience of Luke-Acts. In his explication of this perspective, however, he broadens the ethnic brush by allowing that the writer was either "Jewish, or at least deeply interested in Judaism."[17] This amounts to saying that the author of Luke-Acts was either a Jew or a Gentile. If the latter is taken to be the case, the position is effectively the same as the traditional view.

The universal scope of salvation with its concomitant inclusion of the Gentiles is a widely recognized Lukan theme and long-held tenet in the history of Lukan scholarship. This belief does not prove that the writer was a Gentile, but it certainly fits the perspective one would expect from a Gentile writer. As for the many Semitic expressions and stylistic features reflected in Luke-Acts, such literary characteristics can be explained as the (Gentile!) writer's faithfulness to his Semitic sources. Luke does not write from a detached perspective; he is undeniably a part of the community he describes, and he may well be much more a part of the story he relates than the "we" passages alone suggest.

This brings us to the important consideration of Luke as storyteller. To establish the fundamental presupposition that Luke is not only familiar with but also makes appropriate use of the rhetorical techniques of his day,[18] Parsons enlists the assessment of early pioneers in NT scholarship (B. H. Streeter and Ernst Haenchen) as well as more recent critics (Mark Powell and Robert Tannehill). More significantly,

---

15. Ibid., 15.

16. Admittedly, this effort involves a kind of "hermeneutical spiral," but interpreters gain much from this interplay because, although travel along this path often brings them back to the same place, they arrive there with more insights than they had on the previous visit.

17. Parsons, *Luke*, 7.

18. Ibid., 17.

the author is quick to point out that esteem for Luke's literary acumen is not a recent discovery, but was present *ab ovo*, as the writings of Chrysostom and Jerome testify.

Parsons argues specifically that Luke was familiar with early rhetorical handbooks (*progymnasmata*).[19] Of the four extant handbooks, only one (Theon) is unquestionably early enough to have influenced Luke. The author notes about fourteen topics treated in the *progymnasmata*. Focusing on three (*chreia*, fable, and narrative), he offers selected portions of the Lukan corpus as examples and shows how knowledge of these ancient rhetorical conventions aids our understanding of these passages.

Of particular intrigue is his discussion on the use of inflection in narrative and, in particular, his application of the principle to show that the central figure of the parable of the "prodigal son" is actually the father. Parsons notes that the term "son" is used in the parable almost exclusively in the nominative case, a feature that by his admission "reasonably" points to the subject of the parable. Nevertheless, when read in the light of the progymnasmatic emphasis on the role of grammatical inflection, the fact that the term "father" occurs twelve times, once in all five cases and twice in four cases, cues readers that the central figure of the parable of the "prodigal son" is actually the father.

Of course, Parsons is not the first to suggest the preeminent role of the father in this parable.[20] What's more, his particular argument is neither the only nor the best basis for such a conclusion. For one thing, appealing to the fact that the parable begins and ends with the father (forming a narrative *inclusio*, and thereby suggesting the father's central role) requires fewer and less covert literary data. For another thing, arguing that the father is the central figure of the parable since his verdict puts the terminal period on the assessment of the sins of the sons with a kind of *"ich-habe-geschprachen"* finality also requires no special revelation. Even positing that the fact that Luke has primed the reader to expect that the father will be the central figure of the parable by prefacing it with two briefer, but similar-pointed parables in which non-humans (a coin and a sheep) naturally defer to the seekers (a woman and

---

19. Here Parsons develops points from his previous study, "Luke and the *Progymnasmata*: A Preliminary Investigation into the Preliminary Exercises," in *Contextualizing Acts: Lukan Narrative and Greco-Roman Discourse* (ed. Todd Penner and Caroline Vander Stichele; SBLSymS 20; Atlanta, Ga.: Society of Biblical Literature, 2003), 43–63.

20. See, especially, Eduard Schweizer, *The Good News According To Luke* (trans. David E. Green; Atlanta, Ga.: John Knox, 1984), 247–48.

a shepherd) as the central figures of their respective parables requires no especially keen powers of observation.

These disclaimers notwithstanding, Parsons' argument for the central role of the father in the parable of the "lost sons" based on the known rhetorical strategy of inflection that we see demonstrated in the *progymnasmata* may accurately describe Luke's (Jesus') construction of this particular parable, and may indeed be a helpful hermeneutical tool for understanding other parts of the NT. Nevertheless, in spite of the argument's appeal, Parsons has not demonstrated that the high degree of inflection in the term "father" has resulted from conscious imitation of the progymnasmatic ideal, or whether this phenomenon occurs simply because it was a natural way to tell the story. In any case, these are ostensibly the words of Jesus after all, and even given the appropriate distinction between the *ipsissima verba Jesu* and the *ipsissima vox Jesu*, the evangelists appear not to have played very loosely with the dominical sayings material.

In the final sections of Part One, Parsons uses the *progymnasmata* to explain Luke's motivations for writing, particularly why Luke saw his predecessors' attempts as inadequate. He argues, for instance, that Luke would have seen Mark's "failure" to include details as to Jesus' physical nature (that is, among other things, place of birth, family, etc.) as rhetorically inadequate.[21] Why Parsons leaves unsupported the bald assertion that Luke's "appeal to *eyewitnesses/servants from the beginning* does not serve to insure historical reliability"[22] is not clear. His proposition that the phrase "fit[s] Luke's need to present a narrative, which is, rhetorically speaking, complete" hinges more on the phrase "from the beginning" than on the "eyewitnesses/servants." Surely Luke's use of the term αὐτόπται indicates his concern for historical verifiability,[23] although this does not undermine Parsons' contention that knowledge of rhetorical techniques shared to one degree or another by both Luke and his

---

21. "Failure" and "inadequacy" are perspective-dependent assessments, as the adage "One man's meat is another man's poison" well illustrates. The absence of details surrounding Jesus birth and early childhood in Mark's Gospel may well be a well-planned rhetorical strategy of a different sort. In any case, whether by Mark's conscious construction or the unconscious superintendence of the Holy Spirit, Mark's Gospel refrains from showing Jesus in his weak and vulnerable early years, and this exerts a powerful rhetorical effect on his readers.

22. Parsons, *Luke*, 43 (emphasis mine).

23. On the importance of eyewitness testimony for the historical trustworthiness of the gospel accounts, see the highly acclaimed study of Richard Bauckham, *Jesus and the Eyewitnesses: The Gospels as Eyewitness Testimony* (Grand Rapids, Mich.: Eerdmans, 2006]). Bauckham notes that although the translation "eyewitness" is somewhat misleading since αὐτόπται lacks a forensic sense, the underlying idea is that of a firsthand observer (117).

audience reveals that Luke regarded the efforts of his predecessors as materially or rhetorically inadequate (for his purposes).

Part Two of the book considers Luke as an interpreter of three strands of tradition: pagan, Jewish, and Christian. These are the themes of chapters four, five, and six, respectively. The author's reading of the parable of the friend at midnight in light of the friendship norms of Greco-Roman antiquity offers an interesting exegetical payoff. According to Parsons, Luke's use of φίλος in an oblique case at the beginning and end of the parable alerts the reader/hearer that friendship norms are an important interpretive key. Read in this light, the parable presents a patron who receives a client's request, the denial of which would amount to betrayal of the friendship. In essence, Parsons sees the parable of the friend at midnight as a beacon of hope to those who regarded as betrayal God's apparent inactivity (in terms of deliverance from present trials and suffering) assuring them that "God will not violate the ideals of friendship reciprocity, but will remain a loyal friend."[24]

Two questions arise regarding this approach. The first is this: Is the Hellenistic "friendship" topos *necessary* to convey the notion that God will eventually make good on his promise, or is the Hebraic understanding of "covenant" and God's track-record of faithfulness sufficient to carry this exegetical point?" The answer to this question hinges largely on the distinction between the *Sitz im Leben Jesu* and the *Sitz im Leben Kirche*: the audience of Jesus was largely Jewish; Luke's "primary" audience, most likely an unidentified Roman official of high rank, was Gentile. If the audience is Jewish, or even minimally familiar with Judaism,[25] the answer is "No, it is not necessary" because the notion of "covenant," if not the very epicenter of ancient Israel's faith,[26] surely is a critical foundation stone.

Even though Luke emphasizes the universal demographic scope of the gospel more than other gospel writers, his work has a thoroughgoing Jewish flavor. This is due not only to his concern to represent his sources faithfully, but also to the fact that he understands Christianity to be the true representation of authentic Yahweh-faith. That his first episode has principal characters whose Hebrew names mean "The Lord remembers" (Zechariah) and "the covenant of God" (Elizabeth) adum-

---

24. Parsons, *Luke*, 61.

25. This, of course, could include Theophilus, inasmuch as Luke writes to help him know the "certainty of the things [he had] been taught."

26. The view is championed by Walther Eichrodt, *Theology of the Old Testament* (trans. J. A. Baker; OTL; 2 vols.; Philadelphia, Pa.: Westminster, 1961), 1:17. Significantly, with the single exception of the introductory chapter "Old Testament Theology: The Problem and the Method," every one of the eleven chapters has the word "covenant" in its title.

brates the pericope's theme that Yahweh will live up to the promises of his covenant with Israel. If Zechariah is a synecdoche for ancient Israel, his doubt that Yahweh would answer his long-standing prayer for a son parallels Israel's incipient doubt that Yahweh would answer her long-standing prayer for deliverance from foreign control. Likewise, the joy brought by the birth of Zechariah's son becomes a beacon of hope for the joy that will come via the death of Yahweh's Son, Israel's Messiah. This theme echoes the promise of the Psalmist: "Weeping may remain for a night, but rejoicing comes in the morning" (Psalm 30:5, NIV). Thus, whereas the "friendship" topos would not be necessary for a "covenant-savvy" Jewish audience, for a Gentile audience it may well be an interpretive key.

The assumption that the "friendship" topos is relevant for a Gentile context generates a second question: On what grounds can we conclude that Luke would deem the Hellenistic friendship topos an appropriate grid through which to process the parable of the Friend at Midnight? In favor of Parsons' suggested exegesis is the fact that Luke makes considerable use of the term φίλος.[27] Nevertheless, apart from possibly relating Jesus' own reference to the derogatory epithet "*friend* of tax collectors and sinners," Luke *never* uses the term φίλος in connection with any member of the Godhead.

At first blush, this seems to argue against the hypothesis that Luke intended his audience to process the parable of the Friend at Midnight by means of a "friendship" grid, because the householder is a metaphor for God, and Luke nowhere else uses φίλος in connection with God. However, Luke's reticence to do so likely is due to the ubiquitous undertones of reciprocity that form the basis of the Hellenistic φίλος relationship.[28] Since this is the case, we might expect him to avoid the term completely in connection with God.

But Parsons subsequently demonstrates that Luke has taken up the Hellenistic physiognomic pseudo-science and turned it on its head. Is it possible that Luke (ultimately, Jesus) is doing this very thing with the otherwise enigmatic "though he will not get up and give him, because he is his friend" (Luke 11:7)? To be sure, this is precisely what Luke is doing with Jesus' firm command not to invite to banquet

---

27. Apart from a single reference by Matthew, Luke is the only Synoptic writer to use the term, and he does so fifteen times in his Gospel and three times in the Book of Acts. The only other NT writers to employ the term are James (2 times) and John (8 times).

28. See Gustav Stählin, "φίλος," *TDNT* 9:146–71.

"your *friends*, your brothers or relatives, or your rich neighbors" because of the apparent motivation that they be repaid for their generosity (Luke 14:12). [29]

Parsons completes his treatment of pagan traditions by addressing physiognomy, the ancient, quasi-science of judging inward character traits by observing physical characteristics and mannerisms.[30] According to the author, Luke's account of the healing of the lame man in Acts 3–4 both confirms and overturns typical physiognomic expectations, confirms in that the once weak-in-body-and-moral-fiber man is now standing strong with the bold apostles, and overturns in that his leaping and prancing was misread as a sign of an effeminate or cowardly person. At the very least, this pericope shows the natural reaction of a lame man to the restoration of his limbs as a jubilance that supersedes propriety. The fact that Luke does not shrink back from mentioning the man's leaping and running may be a telling criticism of physiognomic conventions. Surely this is in keeping with Yahweh's words to Samuel regarding Jesse's son Eliab: "Do not consider his appearance or his height, for I have rejected him. The Lord does not look at the things man looks at. Man looks at the outward appearance, but the Lord looks at the heart" (1 Sam 16:7, NIV).

On the other hand, aside from such possible criticism of physiognomic conventions, another point to notice here is that this report of jubilance is quite consistent with a healing of lameness from birth (Acts 3:1–10; 4:22; 14:8), given the long duration of such an illness. A number of symptoms of lameness appear in the background of ancient medicine.[31] Weissenrieder finds that the author of Luke and of Acts can be determined to have had some knowledge of ancient medicine and an interest in healing.[32] The immediate restoration of function in a case such as this lame man could be expected to be an occasion for celebration, given that there would have been absolutely no hope for a cure.

In Chapter Five, Parsons considers Luke as an interpreter of Jewish traditions. For this analysis he selects two specific themes: (1) the city of Jerusalem in the divine economy, and (2) the suffering servant. In the former case, the author argues that

---

29. That this exchange takes place in the house of a Pharisee indicates either the influence of Hellenistic culture, or that reciprocity is an unspoken condition of most human relationships, or both.

30. Readers are treated in this chapter to rich gleanings from Parsons' earlier monograph *Body and Character in Luke-Acts: The Subversion of Physiognomy in Early Christianity* (Grand Rapids, Mich.: Baker, 2006).

31. See Annette Weissenrieder, *Images of Illness in the Gospel of Luke* (WUNT 164; Tübingen: Mohr Siebeck, 2003), 339, 346.

32. Weissenrieder, *Images*, 355–57.

Jerusalem does not occupy "the center of Luke's symbolic world"; rather, it stands as a "beach-head for the Gentile mission."[33] Thus, viewing the Lukan corpus as at least in part a critique of ethnocentric Judaism, we might say that Luke pictures Jerusalem as marking both a terminus and an inception point; Jerusalem represents not only the terminus of an "offshoot religion" that had along critical lines departed from authentic Yahweh-Faith but also the inception of Christianity, the unique expression and torchbearer of that authentic faith *to all the nations*.

Regarding the suffering servant theme, Parsons enlists Luke's inclusion of the conversion of the Ethiopian eunuch to show that the gospel transcends Jewish purity boundaries. His argument is based on the eunuch's social location. Drawing on intertextual echoes between Acts 8 and Luke 24 (where the necessity of the Servant's vicarious suffering is clearly stated), Parsons rebuts Morna Hooker's contention that in Acts 8 Luke intentionally avoided the suffering servant theme by beginning his quotation of Isaiah 53 immediately after the reference to the Servant's vicarious suffering ("The Lord has laid on him the iniquity of us all," v. 6) and ending it immediately before its repeated refrain ("for the transgression of my people he was stricken, v. 8). Moreover, Parsons argues that Luke's precise selection betrays a rhetorical intention to highlight a "humiliation/exaltation schema . . . that is reenacted when the eunuch is baptized by Philip."[34]

Luke's interpretation of Christian traditions is the subject of Chapter Six. In this chapter, Parsons promises to show that Luke has "taken existing material (specifically, "L" parables and Pauline letters) and reworked and reinterpreted that material in the service of his narrative."[35] His case for the Pauline materials is the more compelling.

While Parsons isolates the uniquely Lukan parables and traces out a chiastic structure that emphasizes a reversal-of-fortune theme—a motif that finds multiple echoes throughout the Lukan corpus, he does not show how this is necessarily a "reworking" or "reinterpretation." If these parables were indeed a "collection" that Luke accessed, how can anyone be certain that the order of their presentation in his narrative was entirely a Lukan creation or whether this order was present in the very "collection" that Luke accessed?

Of undeniable significance is the thematic emphasis of reversal and its rhetorical effect. Moreover, while the overall structure of this parable collection emphasizes

---

33. Parsons, *Luke*, 94.

34. Ibid., 107.

35. Ibid., 112.

a reversal theme, each parable makes its own contribution to a proper understanding of the kingdom of God, the character of God, or, in some cases, the Son of God. Here, Parsons is not so much interpreting the parables themselves as identifying the narrative-rhetorical use that Luke makes of them.

Parsons' approach to Luke's interpretation of the Pauline materials takes a different tack. Here he considers the question not from the standpoint of the author, but from the perspective of the authorial audience. Since we are reading the work of a thoroughly-informed and articulate narrative critic, we may assume that by "authorial audience"[36] Parsons means the actual historical flesh-and-blood hearers of Luke's work, not what narrative critics would otherwise distinguish as the "implied" audience. Thus, he asks, "How would an audience familiar with Paul through his letters 'hear' Luke's story of Paul in Acts?" In other words, does Luke reiterate Paul or reinvent him?

Parsons seeks to answer this question by comparing Pauline data gleaned from the book of Acts with corresponding data harvested from the unquestioned Pauline epistles. To accomplish this, he considers Paul along four trajectories: rhetor, miracle-worker, apostle, and theologian.

A particularly compelling part of the author's discussion of Paul as rhetor emerges where he notes no less than four rhetorical strategies that encase the very passage where Paul affirms that he did not come to the Corinthians with "eloquence" (1 Cor 2:1) or "wise and persuasive words" (1 Cor 2:4).[37] Parsons polishes off this argument by citing rhetorical analyses of Paul's speeches in Acts that demonstrate a striking affinity to known rhetorical patterns.

Parsons comes to similar conclusions when viewing the data from the trajectory of miraculous activity. Not only do both the Paul of Acts and the Paul of the epistles work miracles, these miracles are pressed into similar service in both the historical and epistolary contexts: they legitimate God's messenger; they validate the miracle-worker's righteousness; they show the superiority of Israel's God; and they evoke faith.

Using the motif of suffering and the metaphors of laborer and athlete, Parsons again shows an essential continuity between the Lukan Paul and the autobiographical Paul along the apostle-trajectory. The author concludes: "The Acts narrative,

---

36. Ibid., 123.

37. Ibid., 124.

then, develops for the audience what they already know in part from the letters: Paul was right that afflictions are a necessary part of his vocation as an apostle."[38]

In the final part of Chapter Six, Parsons uses concepts of "atonement," "natural theology," and "law" as a grid by which to compare Paul's theology as reflected in the undisputed Pauline epistles with that found in the Book of Acts. Here the author shows that a critical eye for contextual constraints overturns superficial appearances of discord between the Lukan and autobiographical Paul.

According to Parsons, the extent and precision of the parallelism between Acts and the Epistles weighs heavily against limiting Luke's knowledge of Paul to a "general familiarity with some amorphous, oral Pauline tradition."[39] Such precision requires either that Luke was personally and intimately acquainted with Paul or that Luke was thoroughly familiar with his letters.[40] Though many minimize the former, more attention to the collaborative strategies of Paul is warranted. Paul employed amanuenses in the production of his letters. Some of his letters imply a kind of "co-authorship." If Luke was a traveling companion and missionary co-worker with Paul as a natural reading of the "we" passages and the testimony of early Christian witnesses suggest, and if he was as literarily gifted as Parsons and others have demonstrated, then the notions that he truly knew Paul's mind, that he had some degree of influence on Paul, and that he may even have had some level of input into the actual composition of some of Paul's letters are not at all far-fetched.

In the final part of the book, Parsons considers Luke as an evangelist. The term "evangelist" refers specifically to Luke's role as a writer of a canonical Gospel, that is, an approved, authoritative narrative of the words and deeds of Jesus Christ calculated to mediate an encounter between God and its hearers at the point of their deepest need. Depending on the nature of the spiritual "soil" into which this "seed" falls, Luke's narrative offers information, instruction, warning, rebuke, edification, apology, and appeal to conversion.

In the book's final chapter, Parsons sets his sights on Luke's understanding of conversion. As the chapter title suggests, any talk of "conversion" must first deal with the question of what criteria mark a person as a member of "the people of

---

38. Ibid., 134.

39. Ibid., 138.

40. See Paul Elbert's study on this latter probability in light of both ancient literary practice and teaching points in Greco-Roman education from the *progymnasmata*, "Possible Literary Links Between Luke-Acts and Pauline Letters Regarding Spirit-Language," in *The Intertextuality of the Epistles: Explorations of Theory and Practice* (ed. Thomas L. Brodie, Dennis R. MacDonald, and Stanley E. Porter; New Testament Monographs 16; Sheffield: Sheffield-Phoenix, 2006), 226–54.

God"? The author begins his discussion by examining the Lukan corpus for citations from or allusions to the various covenants that Yahweh made with ancient Israel, because covenants establish the "ground rules" for maintaining a relationship. By tracing Jesus' ancestry not to Abraham (so, in reverse chronology, Matthew), but all the way back to Adam, Luke shows that even the Gentiles are related to God.

Although each of the covenants contributes to an overall understanding of what constitutes membership in "God's people," Parsons' primary premise is that Luke saw the Abrahamic covenant as both legitimizing and soliciting a paradigm shift in which the criteria for membership in "the people of God" are reconstituted so as to include Gentiles.[41] For Luke, the Christian movement is for Gentiles a kind of *Statua Libertatis*, welcoming them to transfer allegiance from the kingdom of darkness to the kingdom of light. For Jews, it is an invitation, indeed, a summons to restoration, not a reinvention. As such, Luke's two-volume work is part of an inter-faith dialogue in which Christianity is presented as the only legitimate heir of ancient Israel's Yahweh-faith.

Parsons illustrates Luke's soteriological inclusivism by focusing on the "conversion of Peter, Cornelius, and others."[42] Readers are advised to note that the author carefully distinguishes Peter's experience from the others by labeling it specifically as a "'conversion' to a new point of view, namely, that salvation knows no human boundaries."[43] Nevertheless, the imprimatur on the equal-status admission of Gentiles into the community of faith by this natural born Jew and recognized leader in the Christian community is only part of Luke's rhetorical artistry. By highlighting the soteriological conversions of Lydia, the Philippian jailor, Cornelius—and equally significantly their households—along with the conversions of the Ethiopian Eunuch, Sergius Paulus, and others, Luke has left no doubt that the demographic scope of the People of God is entirely unbounded.

As important as Peter's imprimatur is, readers must not lose sight of the *sine-qua-non* role of the Holy Spirit in soteriological conversion. Although soteriological conversion involves a human transference of allegiance as well as a divine transformation of being, it is entirely a work of the Spirit. Parsons rightly notes the decisive nature of the Spirit's imprimatur. The circumstances surrounding Peter's "sheet vision"—indeed, the vision itself—were clearly orchestrated by the Spirit. But the Spirit's sanction of soteriological inclusivism is nowhere more powerfully demon-

---

41. Parsons, *Luke*, 155.

42. Ibid., 156.

43. Ibid., 157 (interior quotes ['conversion'] his).

strated than in the outpourings of the Spirit on Gentiles. Parson's discussion on the *progymnasmata* in his second chapter may offer some insight here.

Where does Parsons' work lead us in terms of future research? Certainly using the guidelines of early rhetorical handbooks as a grid with which to process the biblical materials, as well as looking at these biblical texts through physiognomic lenses, affords interpreters the opportunity to scrutinize the biblical data from different perspectives, and this almost always engenders some kind of exegetical payoff.[44] More specifically, however, given Elbert's argument of how examples and precedents in the progymnasmatic tradition play an expected literary role in Luke's portrayal of Spirit-reception,[45] I am curious to know whether any other of the rhetorical strategies praised in the *progymnasmata* or evidenced elsewhere in the first-century Hellenistic world might shed further light on the interpretive debate over the doctrines of "subsequence" and "initial physical evidence" with respect to the promised gift of the Holy Spirit to disciple-believer-witnesses at the end of Luke's first book.

In his discussion on the virtue of conciseness as extolled in Theon's rhetorical handbook and modeled to one degree or another in Luke's Gospel, Parsons notes that in the book of Acts Luke has a tendency to repeat material. He refers here to multiple reports of the same episode (notably the twice-told tales of the conversion of Cornelius and the triple recountings of the conversion/call of Saul/Paul). Historical critics for the most part viewed this multiple reporting as not much more than simple redundancy stemming from the literary ineptitude of the writer,[46] but literary critics argue that such repetition is better explained as an author's intentional rhetorical strategy.[47]

---

44. In Chapter Two Parsons cites several studies that demonstrate how reading the biblical materials in light of the rhetorical strategies treated in the *progymnasmata* has yielded valuable exegetical fruit. He emphasizes "fable" as a "relatively untouched" category that, because of its generic similarity to parables, holds promise for biblical interpretation (21–22).

45. Elbert, "Possible Literary Links," 234–37.

46. For example, John C. Meagher, *Clumsy Construction in Mark's Gospel: A Critique of Form- and Redaktionsgeschichte* (New York, N. Y./Toronto: Edwin Mellen, 1979. Meagher's negative assessment of literary features such as multiple reports of the same incident betrays a basic ignorance of ancient narrative devices and rhetorical strategies. This is reflected in the title of Meagher's earlier article "Die Form- und Redaktionsungeschickliche Methoden: The Principle of Clumsiness and the Gospel of Mark," *JAAR* 43 (1975): 459–72. Meagher's title plays on the word *geschichtliche* ("historical") by substituting the term *ungeschickliche* ("awkward," or "unskillful").

47. For example, Leland Ryken (*How To Read The Bible As Literature ... And Get More Out Of It* [Grand Rapids, Mich.: Zondervan, 1984], 59) refers to repetition as "the most reliable guide to what a

Narratologists[48] have long noted that repeated narrative segments—from individual words to entire self-contained episodes—frequently reveal an author's intended themes or concerns. Likewise, Bible scholars have long regarded and utilized repetition as an interpretive cue. In fact, this narrative function is well noticed to have paradigmatic overtones as a recurrent theme in Richard's treatment of the Spirit-reception episodes in the book of Acts.[49] Repetition in the book of Acts is an interpretive clue, suggesting that Luke understands a certain doctrine or practice to be normative for Christians. When something is reported multiple times and in varied contexts in this narrative, it is likely that there is something of eternal relevance being communicated.[50]

A hermeneutical method that is sensitive to repetitive narrative elements is of course not new,[51] but W. E. Nunnally and I acknowledge the formative influence of Stronstad's initial groundbreaking work[52] upon our own teaching on Luke-Acts. Reacting to the overly restrictive and unwarranted exclusion of narrative portions

---

story is about." In oral literature, periodic repetition of the story's antecedent details aids the hearers in keeping track of the plot movement. For a supreme demonstration of this relatively contemporaneous with Luke's narrative achievement, in what may well have been the first ancient romance novel, see Chariton's, *Chaereas et Callirhoe*, passim. For other narrative features of this story, cf. Loveday Alexander, *Acts in its Literary Context* (LNTS 298; London: T&T Clark, 2005), 101–105.

48. For example, Ute E. Eisen, *Die Poetik der Apostelgeschichte: Eine narratologische Studie* (NTOA/SUNT 58; Fribourg/Göttingen: Academic Press/Vandenhoeck & Ruprecht, 2006).

49. Earl Richard, "Pentecost as a Recurrent Theme in Luke-Acts," in *New Views on Luke and Acts* (ed. Earl Richard; Collegeville, Minn.; Liturgical, 1990), 133–49.

50. My former colleague, Waverly E. Nunnally, in his commentary on the book of Acts for on-line courses at Global University, advances a similar theological method that is well suited to narrative interpretation. He suggests that interpretation in Luke's narrative should be attuned to phenomena reported more than once when identifying themes and patterns that stay constant through the changing story of Acts. This narrative-critical hermeneutic is rhetorically valid in determining what Luke expects to be normative realities for the church. A similar hermeneutic is advocated by other scholars, for example, Roger Stronstad, *The Charismatic Theology of St. Luke* (Peabody, Mass.: Hendrickson, 1984), 6–8; J. Scott Duvall and J. Daniel Hays, *Grasping God's Word: A Hands-On Approach to Reading, Interpreting and Applying the Bible* (Grand Rapids, Mich.: Zondervan, 2001), 243; idem, *Journey Into God's Word: Your Guide to Understanding and Applying the Bible* (Grand Rapids, Mich.: Zondervan, 2008), 120–21.

51. For example, Janice Capel Anderson, *Matthew's Narrative Web: Over, and Over, and Over Again* (JSNTSup 91; Sheffield: JSOT Press, 1994).

52. Stronstad, *Charismatic Theology*, 6–8. Stronstad has continued to quantitatively develop a narrative-historical strategy of interpretation, see "The Hermeneutics of Lucan Historiography," in his *Spirit, Scripture and Theology: A Pentecostal Perspective* (Baguio City, Philippines: Asian Pacific Theological Seminary Press, 1995), 31–52; idem, *The Prophethood of All Believers: A Study in Luke's Charismatic Theology* (JPTSup 16; Sheffield: Sheffield Academic Press, ²2003), 13–34.

of Luke-Acts from the interpreters' doctrinal data base,[53] Stronstad subsumes all of Luke's pericopae under one, or a combination, of the following four rubrics: (1) "episodic" (may or may not establish a precedent); (2) "typological" ("looks back to an historically analogous and relevant episode"); (3) "programmatic" ("points ahead to the unfolding of future events"; and (4) "paradigmatic" (expresses a standard "for the mission and character of God's people living in the last days").[54] Of these categories, only the first lacks the repetition element.[55]

Further, analyzing the "outpourings" pericopae under these rubrics secures incontrovertible legitimation for the inclusion of the Gentiles in the people of God, since (1) Luke mentions the phenomenon of *glossolalia* only in contexts of Spirit-baptism; (2) in every case the recipients of Spirit-baptism are believers in Jesus; and (3) Gentiles are Spirit-baptized. Menzies puts the matter this way: "Since according

---

53. On this doctrinally presumed exclusion of authorial didactic intent in the narrative of Luke-Acts, see especially Gordon D. Fee and Douglas Stuart, *How To Read The Bible For All Its Worth* (Grand Rapids, Mich.: Zondervan, 1981), 97, who argue that "*unless Scripture explicitly tells us we must do something, what is merely narrated or described can never function in a normative way*" (italics original, emphasis mine). Fee and Stewart tout an overly restrictive devaluation of the functions of narrative. In addition to the fact that the protasis of their caveat limits the didactic *content* of Scripture to behavioral standards, the notion that didactic *method* be restricted to polished presentations of propositionally-stated, logically-organized postulations that so typify much of Western education overlooks the fact that in Near Eastern culture "narrative" is in fact the instructor's medium of choice. In a revised edition (1993) of *How to Read*, Fee and Stuart added a dubious qualifying phrase to constrain where narrative could serve didactic intent. From their doctrinal data base (no matter the intelligence and competence of an author and active readers), they assert that narrative cannot qualify for didactic function "unless it can be demonstrated *on other grounds* that the author *intended* it to function in this way" (emphases mine).

However, if Parsons, Elbert, and other scholars are right about Luke's familiarity with the *progymnasmata*, we need look no further for "other grounds" to show Luke as a theologian in his own right. Stronstad (*Charismatic Theology*, 8) refers to the notion of the "*purely narrative portions* of Acts" as a "myth"—and he does not have in mind the Bultmannian sense! For Stronstad, the bifurcation of the narratives of Acts into "descriptive" and "didactic" categories is an "artificial and arbitrary . . . dichotomy" (9). In this connection, see also William W. and Robert P. Menzies, *The Spirit and Power: Foundations of Pentecostal Experience* (Grand Rapids, Mich.: Zondervan, 2000), 123–25. Robert Menzies rightly argues that even Fee and Stuart's qualifying stipulation of intentionality is overly restrictive. He writes: "The value of a passage for assessing the theological perspective of a given author cannot be reduced to its "primary intent" (*Spirit and Power*, 124).

54. Stronstad, *Charismatic Theology*, 6–9.

55. Stronstad's last three categories here serve several known functions of repetition in Greek prose style, namely to highlight or draw attention, to establish or fix in the mind of the reader, to emphasize the importance of something, to create expectations, increasing predictability and anticipation, and to build patterns of association (see David E. Aune, *The Westminster Dictionary of New Testament and Early Christian Literature and Rhetoric* [Louisville, Ky.: Westminster John Knox, 2003], 399).

to Luke reception of the Spirit is the exclusive privilege of 'the servants' of God and produces miraculous and audible speech, by its very nature glossolalia provides demonstrative proof that the uncircumcised members of Cornelius's household have been incorporated into the community of salvation."[56]

The primary personal earmarks of Jewish identity were three: regular Sabbath observance, adherence to dietary peculiarities, and circumcision. Jews who became Christians did not immediately forsake any of these activities. Parsons argues successfully that Luke does not portray Christianity and Judaism as "two discrete and separate entities."[57] Both, for example, show continuity with respect to the fulfillment of prophecy. Joel's prophecy and its prophetic extension via the promised gift of the Holy Spirit in the explanatory structure and at the conclusion of Peter's speech at Pentecost (Acts 2:17–18, 38–39) brings the past into continuity with present experience in early Jewish Christianity. In light of the instructive narrative evidence Luke presents, is it not possible that one of the new activities or earmarks of the early Jewish Christians was Spirit-baptism with the accompanying phenomenon of speaking in tongues as Luke describes? The highly unusual nature of glossolalia, especially its superficial resemblance to occult ecstatic experiences and pagan magical incantations, would in part explain the fear-prompted persecution exacted upon early Jewish converts to Christianity.

Parsons's book surely is a most worthy contribution not only to the field of biblical studies, but also to the study of ancient rhetoric. By noting the features of Luke's narrative that appear to reflect awareness and conscious imitation of first-century rhetorical conventions, the author shows that students of Luke will do well to engage these texts with the understanding that their author is every bit as much a theologian as an historian.[58]

---

56. Robert Menzies, in *Spirit and Power*, 127.

57. Parsons, *Luke*, 186.

58. The constructive sense of theologian I have in mind is similar to that advanced in I. Howard Marshall, *Luke: Historian and Theologian* (Exeter: Paternoster, ³1988). Given the thematic emphasis on witness to the ends of the earth assisted by pneumatological experience (Acts 1:8), a witness which original active readers would properly envision as extending beyond narrative time, our understanding of the Evangelist's repeated theological pictures of the great journey of the Way should not be unduly influenced by an often ingrained and unarticulated presupposition of an "apostolic age" or a "Pfingstzeit" in the history of Acts interpretation. This theological understanding of repeated Lukan portraits seems to me the direction of the rhetorically sensitive narrative interpretation that Parsons' analysis would encourage us to pursue.

Gafney, Wilda C. *Daughters of Miriam: Women Prophets in Ancient Israel.* Minneapolis, Minn.: Fortress, 2008. x + 222 pages. Paper. $23. ISBN 978-0-8006-6258-5.

REVIEWED BY LEONARD P. MARÉ

Auckland Park Theological Seminary
Auckland Park, South Africa

Wilda Gafney is Associate professor of Hebrew and Old Testament at the Lutheran Theological Seminary at Philadelphia, and an Episcopal priest. In *Daughters of Miriam: Women prophets in Ancient Israel,* Dr. Gafney has attempted to address a neglected field of research within OT studies, namely the role and function of female prophets in ancient Israel. The book consists of an introduction, followed by six chapters in which she discusses various aspects of the issue at hand.

In the introduction Gafney states the purpose of the book, which is to focus on female prophets as a specific category of professional intermediary religious functionaries in ancient Israel as well as in the Ancient Near East. She then gives a brief overview of how biblical literature portrays what a prophet is and she concludes that women engaged in prophecy in all three parts of the Hebrew canon. It is important to take note that Gafney's definition of what makes a prophet is much broader than is often understood. She describes a wide variety of activities as prophetic (6). This is very important for understanding Gafney's argument, because this reading of the text enables her to identify many more women as prophets, than what usually would be the case.

She then continues with a broad overview of women prophets in modern scholarship, showing that with very few exceptions, it has always been a neglected field of study, with a heavily skewed patriarchal approach to the subject. The introduction concludes with a brief summary of the contents as well as an overview of the rest of the book.

In chapter two the author turns her attention to the subject of biblical prophets and related roles. The simple definition with which she works is that "prophecy is the proclamation and/or performance of a divine word by a religious intermediary to an individual or a community. Such prophetic communication occurred at the instigation of either humans or divinities" (25). She then discusses various technical terms used in the Hebrew Bible for prophet, namely, Man of God, Seer, Visionary, and Judge. The most important part of the chapter is her discussion of the Hebrew root *n-b-'*, specifically as it occurs in the *niphal* or the *hitpael*. In addition to this, she also points out that prophetic activity is often introduced by the phrase *koh amar YHWH*, or by the word *ne'um* or *masa'*, and, in her opinion even the word *mashal* can sometimes indicate prophetic communication. She also argues that because the root *d-r-sh*, which means "to ask, inquire", is almost exclusively used by professional prophets, it denotes a professional practice. This particular argument, to my mind does not hold water. A quick search in a theological lexicon indicates that although the majority of occurrences of this verb indicate prophetic inquiry from Yahweh, there are a number of cases where prophetic activity is clearly excluded. A word only has meaning within its context, and the fact that *d-r-sh* is often used with reference to prophetic inquiry, does not necessarily mean that it always refers to it.

In chapter two Gafney also investigates the phenomenon of female prophecy in the Ancient Near East, where she shows conclusively that female prophets operated not only in Israel, but also in countries around Israel. Chapter three deals with female prophets in the Hebrew Bible, where she discusses the texts referring to Miram, Deborah, Huldah, No'adiah, the anonymous female prophet in Isaiah, the daughters who will prophecy in Joel, and the daughters of the people who prophecy in Ezekiel. Overall, both these chapters are informative and well written.

Chapter four deals with the issue of female prophetic guilds; here she distinguishes between two kinds of guilds, namely musical/funeral guilds and scribal guilds. I do not think that her arguments here, while challenging, are conclusive. At the most one could say that perhaps such guilds existed, but the textual evidence is certainly not conclusive. Her argument that the masculine plural denotes male and female is possible, but certainly not beyond doubt. In chapter five Gafney provides an overview of Rabbinic and Christian trajectories on the subject, a chapter which provides very interesting reading.

The last chapter of her book is to my mind probably the weakest. Her arguments here are to my mind not based on solid exegesis, but I think, she reads too much into the text. Her treatment of Rebekkah inquiring from God as indication of prophetic activity, is too my mind not beyond doubt. Her reading of this text results from her interpretation of the root *d-r-sh*, already referred to above. Her translation and reading of Proverbs 31:1 as an oracle, is too my mind, also highly contentious.

In the end, Gafney's book is a very interesting read. She writes well and is clearly passionate about her subject. I do not always agree with her conclusions and I think that she sometimes reads things into the text that may not be there. However, her book does show that female prophets operated in ancient Israel, and that they possibly were more prominent than what is often believed. One can only hope that the Church at large will take note of this and provide equal opportunities for everyone called by God, whether male or female, to live out their ministry within the Body of Christ.

Davidson, Richard M. *Flame of Yahweh: Sexuality in the Old Testament*. Peabody, Mass.: Hendrickson, 2007. Pp. xvii + 844. Paper. $29.95. ISBN 976-1-56563-847-1.

Reviewed by ROGER D. COTTON

Assemblies of God Theological Seminary
Springfield, Missouri

Richard Davidson and Hendrickson publishers have produced an amazing resource on seemingly every aspect of human sexuality in the OT. The *Flame of Yahweh* is almost encyclopedic in its coverage of the issues. The average page has 1/4 to 1/3 given to footnotes, which are very informative. They include very helpful annotated bibliography of the best sources on each topic or issue. Davidson writes quite clearly and lays out major points of each subject logically and thoroughly. He acknowledges his indebtedness to his mentor, Gerhard Hasel, who was well known as an excellent, conservative, OT scholar. Davidson lets the reader know that he is focusing on the final form of the OT text, and is doing a "close reading," "seeking to understand what constitutes the canonical theological message of the OT regarding human sexuality" (3), with which I totally resonate. I think he does an excellent job bringing out the best reading of the text. Some, whose presupposition is that the text can only be read as a human book and that, sooner or later, we will judge it to have inferior values to our own, will accuse him of putting a positive spin on passages that contradict his ideology. However, I believe scholars and any one else who so accuse Davidson need to admit that they are guilty of, themselves, avoiding some of his conclusions because of their own ideology and presuppositions. I think the evidence of all the Scriptures is in Davidson's favor.

Davidson gives solid studies of ANE parallels at the beginning of each topic and presents the various major scholarly views on each issue, with well-chosen quotations. He lists clearly the major principles he sees, and concludes with what he believes to be the best interpretation. I found myself agreeing with him on every one that I read. On several questions that I have pursued in my own studies his conclusions were almost word for word what I have come to, especially in his Hebrew word studies. Every section has a summary conclusion paragraph which makes the book very readable and useable, after it presents the many, many, detailed arguments. Also, a great feature of every major study is a final section on how God offers grace to people in those situations, with those effects of sin.

The book is divided into three major sections: Sexuality in Eden, covered in two chapters; Sexuality Outside the Garden, spanning ten chapters; and Return to Eden, with two chapters and an afterword relating it all to the NT. Davidson's thesis is "the Edenic pattern for sexuality constitutes the foundation for the rest of the OT perspective on this topic" (3). This is well substantiated throughout the book. The issues dealt with in the middle chapters include: homosexuality, transvestism, bestiality, polygamy, denigration of women (he challenges the common mistaken interpretations), masturbation, premarital sex, divorce, abortion, rape, and others. Each one is dealt with in a very thorough, fair, and sensitive manner, and without coming to extreme positions.

Davidson's conclusion about God's intent for the husband-wife relationship is that it be one of equality without hierarchy. One of the most challenging interpretive issues he deals with is Genesis 3:16 on the husband "ruling over" the wife. His explanation is the most carefully worded and based on the most careful contextual study, that I have seen. The details are too much to be repeated here, but Davidson's idea of leadership in the home involves being a servant and excludes domination. Interestingly, he argues that male leadership over women in the public sphere is not taught or mandated in Scripture (222). In general, Davidson corrects several traditional views that tend to denigrate women, including mistaken understandings of patriarchy, and why women were not allowed to be priests. The latter involves an important principle he sets forth, that, in the OT, God strongly opposes the divinization of sex, as is found in surrounding nations of the ANE (253). His explaining of the story of Esther is the best I have seen, as well as his interpretation of the laws mentioning polygamy, about which he claims "Mosaic legislation condemns all polygamy" (211).

Davidson concludes the book with two chapters on the Song of Songs, which he calls the Holy of Holies of the Scriptures, following Rabbi Akiba. He shows how all the major themes of biblical sexuality he has presented in the book come together in the Song of Songs. The climax is verse 8:6, which he translates as "For love is as strong as death, . . . The very flame of Yahweh" (624), from which he gets the title for his book.

The one totally new interpretation, for me, that I have found so far, in the book, was of the punishment of cutting off the hand of a woman for grabbing a man's genitals in a fight, from Deuteronomy 25:11-12. Davidson makes a very good case that it really referred to shaving her groin area (249), as an appropriate shaming punishment (see the Hebrew word [כף] used there for "hand," 479). This is just one of many, many, enlightening studies he presents. I plan to use this book as a commentary on the verses he deals with, besides as, often, the definitive study on each of his topics.

A thorough bibliography and indices enhance the usefulness of the book.

Waddell, Robby. *The Spirit of the Book of Revelation*. Journal of Pentecostal Theology Supplement Series, 30. Blandford Forum, Dorset, UK: Deo Publishing, 2006. Pp. xii + 228. Paper. £19.95/$24.95/€25. ISBN 90-5854-030-8.

REVIEWED BY DAVID G. CLARK

Vanguard University
Costa Mesa, California

This study is a revision of the author's Ph.D. thesis written at the University of Sheffield. In his Introduction Dr. Waddell holds that the Holy Spirit does play a significant role in the Book of Revelation, even though many scholars have held the opposite view, since the usual New Testament titles "the Holy Spirit," "the Spirit of God," or "the Spirit of Christ" are not used by John. Here, in a brief six pages, the author sets forth his purpose, his methodology ("intertextuality") and the structure of his study. He explains intertextuality as a type of analysis which studies not only the influence of earlier texts upon later texts, but also seeks to discover the effect that later texts have on the interpretation of earlier texts.

In chapter one, "Interpretations of the Role of the Spirit in the Apocalypse: A Survey of Modern Scholarship" (73-8), Waddell finds that discussion is lacking on this topic; no monographs have been dedicated to it and so one must turn to periodicals, book chapters, and theological dictionaries. Within that literature, most scholars interpret the seven spirits of Rev 1:4 as either the seven angels of Jewish angelology or as the Spirit of God. And these scholars generally agree that the other references to the Spirit describe the role of the Spirit as the Spirit of prophecy, and also that the view of the Spirit who indwells every believer is absent in Revelation.

In his longest and quite complex second chapter, "Intertextuality, Revelation, Pentecostalism: The Roundabout of Meaning" (39-96), Waddell now sets out to explain his theoretical framework. He uses the word "roundabout" (the circular intersections common in Britain), because his study will be the intersection where literary theory, studies on Revelation, OT texts, and contextual theology all come together. Then he will apply their contributions to his study of the two witnesses of Rev 11.

Space prevents me from discussing the many topics in this chapter, so I'll list them instead. The chapter opens with the ideological origin (R. Barthes, J. Kristeva; Marxist context) and definitions (various!) of intertextuality, followed by a discussion of the views of S. Fish, chosen because of his work on the significance of text as production. Waddell critiques the views of Fish through J. Culler, bringing J. Derrida, J. L. Austin, E. D. Hirsch, S. Moore, A. C. Thiselton, etcetera into the discussion as well. This section of the chapter concludes with the theological implications of this literary method, emphasizing the relationship between intertextuality and the older method of source criticism.

To his credit, Waddell recognizes that epistemology is the issue here. Those of a modernistic worldview rely on an epistemology of reason, based upon propositional truth(s), while those relying on an epistemology based upon personal experience are said to lean toward a post-modern worldview. Each group will define "text" differently. Irrespective of this assumed worldview dichotomy that Waddell seems to accept, he appears to imply that the latter group, with its particular epistemology which values Christian experience as part of thinking faith, need not uncritically embrace the extreme philosophy of authorial irrelevance. Waddell seems somewhat uncomfortable with the skeptical "postmodern" proposition that meaning is totally independent of the author's control. In any case, when Waddell gets around to his textual analysis that values an epistemology of faith and personal experience, these extreme theories of authorial banishment play no significant role in his interpretive method.

The discussion next turns to a survey of studies in Revelation which have claimed to use intertextuality, although Waddell points out that many of these actually use a more traditional approach. J.-P. Ruiz and S. Moyise do pay more attention to the "situationality of the contemporary reader" and so their work receives the most attention here. G. K. Beale is also included since he offers criticisms of both Ruiz and Moyise. Waddell finds significant agreement with Ruiz and Moyise, concluding (among other things) that the Spirit is the one who interprets Scripture to the community of faith, preferring this communal context (the community is "text" interpreting earlier texts) over the view that Scriptural texts are "self-evident artifacts" that simply need to be dissected by an individual or a scholar, thus minimizing the role of the Spirit and the community.

Chapter two concludes with yet another (brief) discussion which explores some of the reasons scholars recommend the use of the intertextual approach. This might now be augmented by S. Moyise, "Intertextuality, Historical Criticism and Deconstruction," in *The Intertextuality of the Epistles: Explorations of Theory and Practice* (ed. T. L. Brodie, D. MacDonald and S. E. Porter; NTM 16; Sheffield: Sheffield-Phoenix Press, 2006), 24–34. The main point here for Waddell is the importance of a role for a community of readers in the interpretation of texts, not just the intention of the author alone, emphasized by such methods as source and redaction criticism.

In chapter three, "Hearing What the Spirit Says to the Churches: Profile of a Pentecostal Reader of the Apocalypse" (97–131), Waddell has chosen to proceed in a "post-modern direction" where emphasis is placed upon the communal reading of a text. His next task is then to acknowledge and describe his own Pentecostal community. In this way, he hopes to discover a "possible hermeneutic which is faithful to the ethos of the movement" (97).

After briefly summarizing the history of Pentecostalism from its modern beginning at Topeka, Kansas in 1901, Waddell surveys the contributions of various Pentecostal scholars and is able to identify the ethos that guides them, although they use a variety of hermeneutic strategies. Specifically, Pentecostals have a high view of Scripture, and the Spirit that inspired the Scriptures now teaches and transforms readers. But only in the community do we hear what the Spirit is saying to the churches.

Chapter four, "The Faithful Witness of a Pneumatic Church: The Spirit of Prophecy and the People of God" (132–191), turns our attention to the two witnesses of Rev 11:1–13. Waddell first sets out to discover its place within the structure of the book of Revelation. This leads to a discussion of different views of John's structure, and interpretations of such topics as those who are sealed, the trumpets and bowls, the little scroll, and the angels described in chapter ten. He finally concludes that Rev 11:1–13 is the literary center of the book, and also, theologically speaking, "the intertextual center of the role of the Spirit in the Apocalypse" (133).

Given Waddell's Pentecostal ethos as explained in chapter three, he concludes that the role of the Spirit in the Apocalypse is to inspire the prophetic witness of a pneumatic church. The Spirit in the book of Revelation is the Spirit of prophecy. From this position or orientation, he concludes that the identity of the two witnesses is symbolic; they represent the church that bears witness of Christ to the world, and, I might add, suffers greatly for it.

In his "Conclusion: Contributions and Implications" (192–96), Dr. Waddell notes that his summary of literature on the role of the Spirit in Revelation is, so far, the most comprehensive. Next, his attention to "text" also is leading edge to date, as is his study of the passage about the Two Witnesses. Finally, he here offers one of the first Pentecostal strategies of interpretation, with emphasis upon the need for revelation in interpretation and the priesthood of all believers.

The author concludes with a call for a well-developed pneumatology, exploration of the implications of his study for the church and for missions, and more research on John's use of Zechariah (John being the author of Revelation). I would affirm the latter stream of research, and add: more attention to Jesus and Zechariah.

Perhaps it might now be appropriate to offer a brief critique of Waddell's *Spirit in Revelation*. The author is to be commended for his extensive bibliography and his willingness to engage so many sources. Those looking for the origin and development of intertextuality will find help here. But the extensive discussion of this method, not to mention many other subjects, results in less available space for the subject stated in the title. In fact, the title itself is a bit misleading. If someone says "the spirit of the meeting was joyful," "spirit" in this context refers to the prevailing mood or atmosphere. But Dr. Waddell does not mean to determine the prevailing mood of Revelation, but rather the role of the Holy Spirit in Revelation.

I may be mistaken, (and if so I apologize) but this book reminds me of many theses I have chaired where the student chose to use a new methodology learned from a respected professor to interpret some passage(s) of Scripture. What typically results is a study that devotes as much space to the new method as to the interpretation of the passage. Thesis committees often allow this, since the student is devoting time and effort to acquire and use a new methodology. But a more ideal product would result if the student simply stated the method(s) used in the study, gave a brief description of it, and then devoted the majority of the study to the actual use of the method(s).

No doubt Dr. Waddell will protest, saying many prior understandings and contexts needed to be established first, and I'll grant that. Nevertheless, very few pages in this book actually focus upon the Spirit in Revelation, and the key passage of Rev 11.

Speaking of Rev 11 and the Two Witnesses therein, this is indeed a notoriously difficult passage. The Old Testament contains many prophecies pertaining to Israel, and the New Testament church saw itself as the new, spiritual Israel, (not implying that God is done with literal Israel) so that often sorting out passages like Rev 11 becomes next to impossible. Is this prophecy to be taken literally, or figuratively? Pertaining to Israel or to the Church?

Dr. Waddell concludes that the Two Witnesses represent the prophetic ministry of the Church that upholds Christ even during times of persecution. A host of commentators agree with him. But let's have some fun here! Why did John go to such length to specifically recall the miraculous powers of Moses and Elijah, and yet not name the Two Witnesses? What relevance do their unique powers have for the church, unless in the last days the church will be able to call down fire upon its enemies! Is that how Jesus wants the church to spread the good news? So why invoke Moses and Elijah if the church is meant? What if John really did mean the actual appearance of Moses and Elijah?

Didn't Elijah get taken up before death? And what about Moses? The last we see of him is when he ascends Mount Nebo to gaze at the promised land. We're told he's 120 years old, of sharp eye and in good health. So does he just die up there, and if so, of what? But wait, they both appear together on the Mount of Transfiguration! The only two Old Testament characters who spoke with God on Mount Sinai appear on another mountain speaking to Jesus! How did they get there? Well, how did Philip disappear after baptizing the Ethiopian court official and "find himself" at Azotus?

And why are Moses and Elijah talking to Jesus? Luke provides the answer: they are discussing the "exodus" which Jesus was to accomplish at Jerusalem! (Imagine how excited Moses would be to learn about the real exodus from the real enslaver of the world.) Now why do they need to know about redemption through Christ? But then, what other message could God have for the world after the cross? And didn't the Bible say that Elijah would come to reconcile father and son in Israel just before the great and terrible Day of the Lord? Won't the last verse of the Old Testament be fulfilled? And doesn't "Lord" now mean Jesus, and the Day of the Lord his return in power and glory?

Just imagine; a special witness to Israel in preparation for the return of Jesus. With most of the early persecution of the church coming from Jews, it wouldn't be surprising for John to not mention Moses and Elijah by name. Why should God have mercy on those who say they are Jews but are "a synagogue of Satan," and are enlisting Roman help to persecute believers?

Well, we would wish for more dots to connect, but am I the only one who sees a picture coming together here?

In conclusion, Dr. Waddell is a promising young theologian and this book should be an encouragement to budding thinkers within his faith tradition and throughout Christendom who wish to enter the arena of scholarly discussion. But let's remember that as we're inviting the Spirit to speak to our communities through the Scriptures, that the same Spirit also spoke to the original writers and their communities. The original context must never be neglected because the Holy Spirit can use it to speak in appropriate ways or applications to our own times and places. And I'm still wondering if Dr. Waddell needed to be Pentecostal to reach his conclusions, since he cites many others who previously concluded that the Two Witnesses represent the witnessing church.

Twelftree, Graham. *In the Name of Jesus: Exorcism Among Early Christians*. Grand Rapids, Mich.: Baker, 2007. Pp. 351. Paper. $26.99. ISBN 978-0-8010-2745-1.

REVIEWED BY JON MARK RUTHVEN

Boise, Idaho

Graham Twelftree's new work, *In the Name of Jesus: Exorcism among Early Christians* follows on an interest in exorcism he begun as early as 1980 ("Demon-Possession and Exorcism in the New Testament," with James D. G. Dunn, *Chm* 94 [1980], 210–25). This theme appeared in his revised doctoral dissertation, *Christ Triumphant: Exorcism Then and Now* (London: Hodder and Stoughton, 1984) and later in *Jesus the Exorcist: A Contribution to the Study of the Historical Jesus* (Tübingen: Mohr / Peabody, Mass.: Hendrickson, 1993). This theme appears as well as in a number of articles.

With all this, Twelftree's productions scarcely intrude on a crowded field: academic interest and attitudes toward exorcism in the NT have rarely been shaped by the orthodoxies of respect for worldviews that are not philosophically hatched in a white-male Eurocentric matrix. So even today, according to the author, exorcism remains a "superstition," requiring a stern demythologizing.

To his credit, Twelftree courageously engages this shunned subject, moving beyond mere apologetics to his "chief aim" to "determine the place" and "describe the practice of exorcism among early Christians." He attempts to further explain the "variety of approaches" to exorcism in the NT canon (29). The place of exorcism is so essential to Christianity that the practice expresses its nature and "the various understandings of its mission," its "theological diversity," particularly as it relates to the "various ways" Jesus the exorcist as a "model" was understood by the differing traditions within Christianity. The "plan of attack "in this work is to "set out a brief general description of exorcism and exorcists of the period including that associated with Jesus." The author does so to lay out the variety of exorcistic practices with a view to compare and contrast the distinctive elements without and within the

Christian community. Beginning chronologically, the NT is then examined for "each writer's view on the place and practice of exorcism," views which are then brought into "sharper relief" by the Apostolic Fathers, the apologists, the longer ending of Mark, and even the earliest critics of Christianity: Celsus, Lucian of Samosota, and Galen (32–33). Twelftree then prosecutes his project with a meticulous examination of the textual evidence.

The problem is not the scope of this project and certainly not its subject matter, but, in this reviewer's opinion, the writer's hermeneutic. First, quite broadly, while it can be interesting to trace the development (or devolution) of NT themes into the second century, Twelftree's approach of testing, or at least drawing these themes into "sharper relief" seems to imply an underlying Darwinian or Hegelian "progress of doctrine" model which apparently denies that the Church, over the centuries, "progressed" right into the Dark Ages. At the risk of appearing culturally insensitive or biblicistic, on my reading, the early church fathers thought and wrote demonstrably out of their depth compared to the profundity and sophistication of the NT. Hence, it seems (to me) odd to structure this project around the expectation that those in the second century, far removed from the immediacy, accuracy and spirit of the first witnesses of Jesus, could serve as arbiters of truth about apostolic faith and practice.

Perhaps this hermeneutical valuation makes sense if the NT, particularly the Gospels, are rejiggered, via higher critical emendations, so as to lose their explicit message and thereby, their authority. For example, in discussing the crucial commissioning accounts in Matt 10 and Luke 9 "we arrive at the conclusion that we have no direct evidence that Jesus charged his disciples with performing exorcisms." Why? Since the explicit commands of Jesus for exorcism are possibly derived from Mark (6:7), the explicit parallel passages, Matt 10:8 and Luke 9:1, cannot be used as evidence for Jesus' commands to not only heal but to exorcize! Not even the evidence at the end of the second pre-Easter commissioning of the Seventy (72) in Luke 10:17 is sufficient: "... it is highly unlikely that he [Luke] would have dropped a reference to it if it had been in his tradition of the charge" (50–51).

Along this line, we read other puzzling observations. For example, when Twelftree contrasts the practices of Jesus against those of contemporary exorcists he suggests that "apart from the exorcism, Jesus expresses no interest in control of, and protection from unwanted demons" (48). To be fair, he notes the "story of the returning spirit" (n. 65) that offers a prescription against re-possession; this is actually spelled out by Twelftree on pages 96–98 and 169–70. Does this suggest, again, that the "real" historical Jesus was also unaware of these sayings attributed to him by Matthew and Luke? It seems that the recovery of the "historical Jesus" requires a stringent and unjustifiable jettisoning of many Gospel texts purporting to describe him. Does even secular historiography impose such skepticism on its primary sources?

This premise seems to underlie another puzzling assertion: "at no point did any of the traditions seek to attach the practice of prayer to Jesus' exorcistic technique." On what hermeneutical ground were the logia omitted that are recorded in Mark 9:29 – Matt 17:21 ("fasting" added)? Page 124 affirms that "prayer is effective in exorcism" in the context of Mark 9:29. If so, why is this denied as evidence for the claim, above? Apparently, because we are discussing Mark here, and not attempting to sift evidence for the "historical Jesus." As we have seen in the previous example, Matt 17:21 is recused on the ground that it was derived from Mark! Similarly, Twelftree argues that though Jesus may have used the language of exorcism against a storm (Mark 4:39) "he did not appear to rebuke sickness, reserving exorcistic language and technique for the removal of demons" (48). It appears that the identical word for "rebuke" (ἐπετιμάω) against a fever in Luke 4:39 is similarly disqualified as evidence.

Still again: "we look in vain for evidence that Jesus asked or expected his followers to be exorcists after Easter" (54). Does the prominent "Great Commission" not apply here, in which a clear echo of the earlier commissioning accounts regarding "authority" (ἐξουσία) of Jesus over demons "given" them? Would not the appropriation of ἐξουσία over demons be part of "everything I have commanded you"?

This work also seems to offer an easy equivalence of non-Christian and Christian "magical exorcists" ("not pejorative" terms, we are assured!). This supposed descriptive equivalence is "based not so much on their personal force [as that of Jesus] as on engaging an outside power-authority" (53). However, the Evangelists clearly do not understand Jesus as a magician. Does their voice count? Do they deserve to be shrouded with the radical philosophical presupposition of authorial irrelevance? The logic here is very much like the late William Buckley's observation about liberals' moral equivalence of the KGB and the CIA using "similar practices": It "is the equivalent of saying that the man who pushes an old lady *into* the path of a hurtling bus is not to be distinguished from the man who pushes an old lady *out* of the path of a hurtling bus: on the grounds that, after all, in both cases someone is pushing old ladies around." While the NT tries to be accommodating to non-Christian exorcists (Mark 9:38 – Luke 9:49), it nonetheless demands clear discernment of their sources and purposes (Mark 3:22–29; Acts 19:14–17).

The process of prosecuting the thesis that there were a variety of early Christian traditions about exorcism should involve a transparent historiography. Twelftree's campaign to re-establish healing and exorcism to their rightful place in Christian praxis is commendable, but if one is to convince skeptics steeped in old Enlightenment methodologies, it seems odd to use a strategy of collusion with those same methodologies, since they easily can produce the same subjective, ahistorical skepticism with which they began. Because of a self-imposed, hypercritical historiography, one a-priori premise is that Jesus simply cannot appear as he does on the pages of the Gospels.

This most recent third quest for the "historical Jesus," marginally different in spirit from the previous quests, again relies on a higher critical hermeneutic with roots in untested philosophical speculation about the existence of objective truth in reality and history and anachronistic debates pertaining thereto. This ideology clearly reaches beyond the pale of traditional Evangelicalism. Certainly this questionable path toward understanding intelligent and competent authors is a personal and institutional choice, but will it ultimately lead to an encounter with, not only the historical, but the living Jesus?

Fee, Gordon. *Galatians*. Pentecostal Commentary Series. Blandford Forum, Dorset, UK: Deo Publishing, 2006. Pp. ix + 262. Paper. $34.95/€35/£24.95. ISBN 978-1-905679-02-7.

REVIEWED BY JANET MEYER EVERTS

Hope College
Holland, Michigan

As Fee acknowledges in his introduction, writing a fresh commentary on Galatians is a daunting task. Almost everyone who teaches the New Testament in college or seminary includes it in introductory New Testament courses and Galatians stands as the backbone of every Pauline Literature course. From the time of the Reformation to the present, Protestants have followed Luther and claimed Galatians as the basis of their theology of justification by faith. There is little doubt that Galatians is one of the most interpreted and over-interpreted books in the New Testament.

This author, however, is more than capable of meeting the challenge of writing a commentary on Galatians that does more than rework the material of others. His commentary offers new perspectives on this important letter of Paul and does so in a way that is not only properly sensitive to Spirit-related issues in interpretation, but also displays careful attention to textual details.

As he states in the introduction to the commentary, Fee wants to help people read Galatians as though the Reformation had never happened. This, of course, is actually an impossible task. What Fee means is that he wants to offer a perspective that differs substantially from a standard Reformation reading of Galatians. Fee claims that Galatians is not about how one *enters* into relationship with Christ—whether by faith in Christ or by works of the Law—but about how that life in Christ is brought to completion. From his perspective the question of Galatians is: *Does one need to add Torah to be completed in Christ?*

This is the question that controls Fee's reading of the entire book of Galatians. He understands the first two chapters as Paul's argument to establish his independence from Jerusalem and the truth of the gospel he preaches. The truth of Paul's gospel and the examples from his experience become the basis for his argument in Gal 3:1–6:10 that in the continuing life in Christ, the Spirit, not Torah, plays a major role. This is the major thesis of Galatians. In Gal 3:1–5, Paul's appeal to the Galatians' experience of the Spirit is part of his argument from scripture because he wants them to understand how they fit into Israel's story as Abraham's heirs. Christ's death is the end of the Law and the Galatians' experience of the Spirit confirms that the gift of the Sprit is real since they know the indwelling empowering Spirit in their lives. Fee's treatment of Gal 3:27 brings many of his distinctive emphases into focus. People *enter* the Christian life and participate in Christian baptism on equal footing regardless of human distinctions—this is quite unlike circumcision which was only for males and Jews. But it is also vital that they continue to live by the Spirit in Christ. Circumcision is *anathema* because it takes people back to the Law and keeps boundaries intact—Gentiles are forced to be Jews and women are excluded. For Paul: "Christ and the Spirit have eradicated and transcended such nonsense" (143).

Fee's understanding of the argument of Galatians is especially helpful in connecting Gal 5:13–6:10 to the theological body of the epistle. This passage has usually been understood as reflecting a major shift from thinking theologically about the gospel to giving ethical instruction. Fee suggests that it is much better understood as bringing the argument of Galatians to a close: "Having begun with the Spirit are you ending with the Flesh?" No, says Paul, you come to completion by living in the Spirit. The Spirit alone is both the replacement for the Law and the antidote to the works of the Flesh. The great strength of Fee's commentary is that he is able to present the internal consistency and logic of Galatians as a whole. He sees the letter as Paul's argument for living in the Spirit as a Christians and is able to show Paul's readers the power of this argument.

The overall strength of Fee's commentary does not mean it is without weaknesses. I found the most glaring to be his understanding of Paul's use of scripture in Galatians. Fee suggests that scripture played an important part in Paul's argument because it played a crucial part in his opponent's arguments. The reason why modern readers find Paul's scriptural arguments so difficult to follow is that he is responding to his opponent's arguments. Fee then tries to reconstruct the arguments of Paul's opponents and suggests that the questions of "Who are Abrahams true children?" and therefore "Who are heirs of the promise?" was the issue for Paul's opponents who were arguing from Genesis 17. Paul answers them from Genesis 15. I found this reconstruction speculative at best and rather unconvincing. There is no indication in Galatians that his opponents were mentioning Abraham at all and Abraham is a key figure for Paul in Romans as well. In light of Acts 15, the Law of Moses was at issue in the Council of Jerusalem and the Law of Moses is certainly what Paul is referring to in the latter half of Galatians 3. It seems more likely that Paul is using Abraham and the covenant with Abraham in both Galatians 3 and 4 to trump Moses and Mosaic covenant than that he is using Genesis 15 to trump Genesis 17.

There are also some specific strong points that are evident in this commentary relating to its academically independent nature. For example, this is immediately clear in the introduction when Fee admits that "it is currently unpopular for an Evangelical scholar to do so" (4), but still dates the letter *after* the Council of Jerusalem. He points out that equating Acts 15 and Galatians 2 is a matter of simple math and in the commentary proper points out that the subject of circumcision is the explicit subject matter of both chapters as well. What a relief for those of us, both Evangelicals and Pentecostals, who find the conservative Evangelical arguments equating the Galatians 2 visit with Acts 11 so embarrassing!

When Fee comments on Gal 3:1–6, he is not afraid to point out that Paul is appealing to the Galatians *experience* of the "*initial reception* of the Spirit as proof positive that their new life in Christ is predicated on faith" . . . "which in turn leads to an appeal to their *present experience* of the Spirit and his miraculous activity in their midst" (103). All this contextual recognition of an emphasis on experience and the miraculous and continuing activity of the Spirit is hardly typical of the standard perception of Paul in the Protestant commentary tradition on Galatians. At the same time Fee avoids becoming embroiled in the Evangelical Protestant/Pentecostal controversy as to whether Paul is referring to a subsequent "Spirit baptism" here (quotation marks his), although other scholars, independent of ecclesiastical affiliations, would simply describe this discussion about the language of Gal 3:2 (τὸ πνεῦμα ἐλάβετε) with respect to the identical language in the book of Acts as both a valid socio-rhetorical and intertextual topic, the correlation with events in Acts having been suggested by a number of critical commentators (Hans Dieter Betz's *Galatians*, for example). In any case, Fee does not engage this discussion here, which might distract from his focus on appraising the strong Pauline witness to the continuing and miraculous activity of the Spirit in the life of faith.

This commentary also contains two sections of vintage Fee in which Fee the scholar manages to summarize a complex issue into a few short paragraphs. At least one of these summaries, the discussion of the use of πίστις + Χριστοῦ (84–88) is worth the price of the commentary. Here Fee answers what he calls the "groundswell" of New Testament scholarship which wants to see this as a reference to Christ's faithfulness rather than faith in Christ. Fee concludes that the "traditional" meaning of "faith in Christ," as long as "faith in Christ" means "trusting wholly in Christ" and not just assenting to something one believes to be true, is certainly the correct way of understanding *pistis xristou* (88). Then, in the introduction, there is a summary of the role of the Holy Spirit in Galatians that is not technical but is a short and thorough summary of a complex issue (7–9). Both of these sections are vintage Fee and duly reflect this author's Pauline expertise.

In conclusion, Fee's commentary on Galatians is a sterling addition to an emerging new series which is written for pastors and educated lay persons and is not meant to be highly technical. Yet Fee has skillfully presented a good deal of current scholarship in highly understandable and relevant terms. He does a marvelous job of connecting the role of the Spirit in Galatians to the central theme of the letter. What could be both more Pentecostal and more applicable to global Christianity than this?

REVIEWED BY GEORGE LYONS

Northwest Nazarene University
Nampa, Idaho

Preachers and even some professors seldom use commentaries as they do other books, except for dictionaries and encyclopedias. As a rule, they do not read commentaries, they consult them. They generally work primarily with the biblical text and refer to commentaries only as they encounter interpretive problems calling for explication. Then they consult as many commentaries as they can in an effort to resolve these problems.

Consequently, few commentary users have a comprehensive sense of how commentators deal with a book as a whole. There are both advantages and disadvantages to this approach to commentary use. Professor Fee's commentary is not particularly conducive to consulting. It reads much more like an engaging book than the collections of word studies, grammatical discussions, background information, and arguments with previous commentators that are typical of the commentary genre.

One of its noteworthy features that makes Fee's commentary eminently readable is that it shares few of the expected features of typical commentaries. Read it alongside his NICNT commentary on *1 Corinthians* and the differences become obvious.

Footnotes are comparatively few and seldom list a succession of scholarly opinions for or against a particular reading of a controversial passage. But Fee does not avoid controversy. For example, he ably critiques and finally rejects the recent scholarly preference for taking the "faith of Christ" (in Gal 2:16 [2x], 20; 3:22) as a subjective genitive (i.e., as Christ's faithfulness to God).[1]

Fee's *Galatians* commentary is totally unpretentious. Its bibliography mentions only the more enduring English-language commentaries on Galatians. But Fee's thorough familiarity with Galatians scholarship is obvious. His long experience as an exegete and churchman shines through, despite the commentary's easy accessibility. This is not a commentary intended for scholars only. Average readers will profit from the good sense and sound exegetical judgment demonstrated throughout.

Far too many commentary series seem preoccupied with antiquarian and esoteric interests alone. Fee and the Pentecostal Commentary series are to be commended for their serious attempt to engage contemporary readers with the continuing relevance of the scriptural text.

Each of the major sections of the commentary concludes with a reflection and response. These bring together theological and practical implications of interest to contemporary Christians. The response sections make it next to impossible to read the letter as a merely curious archaeological artifact.

Readers of *JBPR* may be particularly interested in Fee's treatment of the Spirit in Galatians. He does not allow his Pentecostal heritage or the series to bias his exegetical judgment. Nonetheless, he explicitly spells out the implications of Paul's law-free gospel for "present-day Pentecostal and evangelical churches." Thus, for example, he challenges the inconsistency of those who exclude "Spirit-gifted women . . . from functioning with their gifts in the community of faith."[2]

Fee consistently focuses far more on the communal than on the individual experience of the Spirit. He understands Gal 3:5 to refer to "God's supply of the Spirit in their community life,"[3] expressed by "a variety of supernatural phenomena."[4] He summarizes the message of Gal 3:1–14: "the Galatians' common reception of the Spirit has in effect brought Torah observance to an end, since the aim of the law is

---

1. Gordon Fee, *Galatians*, 84–88.
2. Ibid., 198.
3. Ibid., 111.
4. Ibid., 112.

now written on the heart and thus fulfilled through the gift of the Spirit."[5] Although a variety of commentators read Gal 3:2–5 as referring to the experience of the Spirit as subsequent to conversion,[6] Fee insists that: "Individual conversion history is simply not in view here."[7] He considers Gal 5:24–25 one of the most significant in the Pauline corpus for our understanding of Pauline ethics, as Spirit-empowered Christlikeness, lived out in Christian community in loving servanthood. At issue is not a Spirit-flesh struggle within the believer's heart, but the sufficiency of the Spirit for life in the believing community—over against both the law and the flesh, as God's replacement of the former and antidote to the latter.[8]

For all of the distinguishing assets of Fee's commentary, it is flawed by the same questionable historical and methodological assumption typical of modern treatments of Galatians: mirror reading. Until recently, interpreters have imagined they could reconstruct the arguments of Paul's Galatian opponents by simply reversing his assertions and denials in the letter. They arbitrarily presume that Paul's opponents assume what he denies and / or deny what he asserts. The procedure is arbitrary since no interpreter does this for every Pauline assertion and denial in the letter.

---

5. Ibid., 124.

6. Among scholars who suggest this probability, see Hermann Gunkel, *The Influence of the Holy Spirit: The Popular View of the Apostolic Age and the Teaching of the Apostle Paul* (trans. Roy A. Harrisville and Philip A. Quanbeck II; Philadelphia, Pa.: Fortress, 1979), 17, 91.

7. Ibid., 153. {Fee's definite insistence that Paul and his readers would not have understood the spiritual history of Spirit-reception by faith and Spirit-experience mentioned at Gal 3:1–5 may be distinctive. Of course if Paul's language of faith (Gal 2:16b) is automatically synonymous with his Spirit-reception language, as Fee and Protestant theology in general tend to assume in reading Paul, then "individual conversion history" does not exist. Other scholars take a more nuanced approach as to Paul's probable meaning here. Some note that the experience referred to in vv. 2, 5 is not clear ("nicht eindeutig" [François Vouga, *An die Galater*, HNT 10; Tübingen: Mohr Siebeck, 1998], 68), while others suggest inferences from early Christian history. The latter reading cannot possibly be dismissed as the product of "some Pentecostals" (so, Fee, *Galatians*, 106, n. 6). While we can expect that Paul thought his original addressees would easily grasp his intended meaning based upon their remembrance of his previous teaching and of their past experience, later readers might well appreciate rhetorical clarification. In his discussion of "3,1–5 Erinnerung an die Erfahrung des Geistes," Vouga, for example, is therefore content to observe that "der Glaube nicht auf den Geist zurückgeführt wird, sondern daß der Geist die Gabe ist, die der Galube empfängt (Gal 3,2.5; 4.6)" and that linguistically "Der Aor. ἐλάβετε V. 2 bezog sich auf die geistige Geschichte der Galater" (65–69 [68, 69]). Fee's insistence, to the effect that Paul would not expect his original readers to be mindful of or have in view remembered experiences (*die geistige Geschichte*) described by his Spirit- and power-language at Gal 3:2–5, 14b, perhaps demands more than the textual evidence actually allows.} — Ed.

8. Ibid., 201.

In this sense, Fee's commentary stands in the tradition of F. C. Baur[9] and the Tübingen School.[10] Like nearly all interpreters of Galatians since the nineteenth century, he assumes that Paul's letter responds to specific accusations made by invading Judaizing opponents. Typically, commentators imagine that in Galatians Paul defends his independence from the Jerusalem apostles against the charge that he was dependent on them (by mirror reading 1:1 and 11–12). And / or, they claim that Paul denied the charge that his gospel compromised that of the original apostles in order to make it more appealing to his Gentile audience. On both assumptions, Paul's opposition allegedly forced him to defend the divine origin of his apostleship against charges that it was illegitimate (by mirror reading 1:10).[11] Fee takes this scholarly consensus for granted in his reading of Galatians.[12]

But this is an assumption, not a conclusion. All we can know about Paul's Galatian opponents must be surmised from his rhetorically exaggerated, even distorted characterizations of them. It may be that the designation "opponents" is inappropriate. Certainly, Paul opposed some he identified as troublemakers and perverters of the gospel. But it is not certain whether the opposition was mutual or only from Paul's side, whether the intentions of the "opponents" were malicious or well-meaning, whether they understood Paul's position correctly or not, whether Paul fully grasped their position, whether they came from inside or outside the Galatian communities, whether the traditional designation "Judaizers" is appropriate or not, and whether or not they had ties to Jerusalem. Like most modern commentators on Galatians, Fee's reading of the letter depends on unproven and unprovable conjectural hypotheses. Whether a commentary on Galatians free of such hypotheses can be helpful and persuasive remains to be seen.[13]

---

9. Ferdinand Christian Baur, *Paul the Apostle of Jesus Christ: His Life and Works, His Epistles and Teachings* (ed. Eduard Zeller; trans. A. Menzies from the ²1845 edition; 2 vols. in 1; Peabody, Mass.: Hendrickson, 2003), 1:260–67.

10. See Werner Georg Kümmel, *The New Testament: The History of the Investigation of Its Problems* (trans. S. McLean Gilmore and Howard C. Kee; Nashville: Abingdon, 1972), 120–84.

11. Among those who have called the scholarly consensus into question are: Franz Mussner, *Der Galaterbrief* (HTKNT 9; Freiburg: Herder, 1974), 11–29; George Howard, *Paul: Crisis in Galatia. A Study in Early Christian Theology* (SNTSMS 35; Cambridge: Cambridge University Press, 1979), 1–7; George Lyons, *Pauline Autobiography: Toward a New Understanding* (SBLDS 73; Atlanta: Scholars Press, 1985; repr. 2008), 75–121; Frank J. Matera, *Galatians* (Sacra Pagina 9; Collegeville, Minn.: Michael Glazier / Liturgical Press, 1992), 7, 47–48, 54.

12. Fee, *Galatians*, 12–15, 34–38, 114–15, 197.

13. See George Lyons, *Galatians* (New Beacon Bible Commentary; Kansas City: Beacon Hill Press), forthcoming, 2010.

The *Journal of Biblical and Pneumatological Research* is indexed and/or abstracted by the following services: *Index Theologicus* (Universitätsbibliothek Tübingen, (www.ixtheo.de); *Old Testament Abstracts* (Catholic University of America); *New Testament Abstracts* (Boston College School of Theology and Ministry); *Religion and Theological Abstracts* (www.rtabstracts.org); and the *Religion & Philosophy* and *Academic Search Complete* databases from EBSCO.

Notes for Contributors to JBPR

Submissions should be made by e-mail attachment in the format of a Microsoft Word document.

- Submissions should be double spaced, and include a cover page, with the title of the article and author's name.

- The article itself should not include the name of the author, nor any self-reference to the author via statements like "See my previous study...," or "As I have argued in...," whether in the body of the essay nor in its footnotes.

- Footnotes should be used, not endnotes. Footnotes should be double spaced. Bibliographies and reference lists are not allowed.

- Whether in articles or in reviews, *JBPR* will not discriminate on the basis of the number of words. Content, not length, will be paramount in the editorial and peer-review process.

- *JBPR* will employ SPIonic and SPTiberian fonts, respectively, for Greek and Hebrew characters. These two font sets may be downloaded from the following web-site: http://www.sbl-site.org/educational/BiblicalFonts_SPlegacyFonts.aspx.

- The en-dash (–), rather than a hyphen, should be used between page numbers, verses, and dates. (For example, Gen 1:1–2:3 illustrates the en-dash.) Between phrases in a sentence, where appropriate, use em-dashes (—), not hyphens.

- Full pagination spread must be used when citing a journal article or an essay in a collection. A specific page in the work so cited should be indicated by the page placed in parentheses. Examples of these two instances are as follows: Margaret E. Dean, "Textured Criticism," *JSNT* 70 (1998): 79–91 (82), and Ronald F. Hock, "Homer in Greco-Roman Education," in *Mimesis and Intertextuality in Antiquity and Christianity* (Studies in Antiquity & Christianity; ed. Dennis R. MacDonald; Harrisburg, Pa.: Trinity, 2001), 56–77 (58).

- On all other specific guidelines of style and format, consult Patrick H. Alexander et al., eds., *The SBL Handbook of Style for Ancient Near Eastern, Biblical, and Early Christian Studies* (Peabody, Mass.: Hendrickson, 1999). This handbook of style is available on-line at http://www.sbl-site.org/assets/pdfs/SBLHS.pdf.

www.ingramcontent.com/pod-product-compliance
Lightning Source LLC
Chambersburg PA
CBHW080436230426
43662CB00015B/2294